S UPPLEMENTARY
E MPIRICAL
T EACHING
U NITS in
P OLITICAL
S CIENCE

Political Socialization Across the Generations

Developed By
PAUL ALLEN BECK
University of Pittsburgh

JERE W. BRUNER
Oberlin College

L. DOUGLAS DOBSON
Northern Illinois University

We would like to acknowledge our gratitude to Professor M. Kent
Jennings of the Center for Political Studies at the University of
Michigan for making the 1973 portion of this study available to us
before he has completed his analysis of it. These data are to be used
for teaching purposes only, and the weights which make them a
representative sample have been omitted.

Revised Edition, August, 1975
(The test edition was entitled "Political Socialization: Inheritance and
Durability of Parental Political Views")

The American Political Science Association
1527 New Hampshire Avenue, N.W.
Washington, D.C. 20036

The development of SETUPS, a series of learning materials on topics in American Politics, was supported by Grant GZ 3442 from the National Science Foundation to the American Political Science Association. This grant supported a College Faculty Workshop, hosted by the Inter-University Consortium for Political Research, at the University of Michigan, Summer, 1974.

The Workshop Project was administered by the Association's Division of Educational Affairs. The Workshop implemented a recommendation by the Task Force on Computer Related Instruction and approved by the Steering Committee on Undergraduate Education, to the effect that support should be sought to facilitate the development of learning materials that involve political science students actively in inquiry.

Test editions of SETUPS were prepared by the faculty participating in the workshop. (Seven of these test editions were prepared and distributed initially by the ICPR project staff.) Each SETUPS was reviewed by at least three qualified persons and tested in at least six classes. These evaluations were used by the authors and the editor in revising the modules.

The revised editions of SETUPS are published under the auspices of the Division of Educational Affairs. However, the views expressed are those of the authors and not of the Division of Educational Affairs or of the American Political Science Association.

TABLE OF CONTENTS

FOREWORD

Throughout its history, the American Political Science Association has been interested in teaching. A standing committee on teaching political science was appointed at the first organizational meeting of the APSA in 1903. At the second meeting of the newly formed association in 1905, the principal report delivered to the members was on a survey of college freshmen, conducted by William Schaper of the University of Minnesota, called "What Do Our Students Know About American Government Before Taking College Courses in Political Science?" Since then, APSA has been almost continuously engaged in one or more activities designed to assist teachers. These early activities are summarized in a 1963 report on the history of Association education activities by Cora Prifold (Beebe). In all of this activity, the Association has been concerned that its efforts not establish an orthodoxy, a preferred method or approach. It has and does seek to aid teachers with diverse interests, fields and techniques.

SETUPS is another in the long list of efforts to aid teachers. The Association's role in their production and distribution grows out of the recommendations of a Task Force on Computer Related Instruction, established in February, 1973, which reported to the Steering Committee on Undergraduate Education in January, 1974. The latter committee agreed that there was a need for special learning materials for data analysis exercises and simulations.

At this point, APSA was fortunate in receiving a grant from the National Science Foundation's College Faculty Workshop Program that enabled DEA to develop the SETUPS with cooperation of the Inter-University Consortium for Political Research. A workshop was held, at the University of Michigan, Betty Nesvold and William Buchanan serving as coordinators.

We owe a debt of appreciation to the individual authors who were ultimately responsible for the written materials and to the schools that participated in the testing program. After testing, each booklet was revised for publication.

It is the hope of those who have participated in the project that the materials will prove of value to many teachers. It also is hoped that the Association will be able to continue to meet these needs while at the same time aiding in the development of other projects to assist teachers in other areas of the discipline having different theoretical and pedagogical perspectives.

Evron M. Kirkpatrick
Executive Director
American Political Science Association
August, 1975

v

EDITOR'S PREFACE

Supplementary Empirical Teaching Units in Political Science are modules for teaching American government. Their function is to stimulate students to independent, critical thinking, to convey a deeper understanding of portions of the substantive content of the course, and to demonstrate how scholars accumulate the evidence and reach the conclusions that appear in their textbooks. They enable students to make use of the computer with no previous training, either to analyze data on political behavior or to see the consequences of policy decisions by use of a simulation model.

They were developed by a group of political scientists with experience in teaching the introductory American Government course who were brought together in a workshop supported by a grant from the National Science Foundation in the summer of 1974. The American Political Science Association administered the grant, and the Inter-University Consortium for Political Research was host to the workshop and provided data for most of the SETUPS. Seven modules were then tested during the 1974-75 academic year in 155 classes in 69 universities and colleges, and evaluated by their students and faculty. The revised editions were based upon this experience. Additional SETUPS in American Politics and Comparative Politics are now in the process of development.

Participants in the 1974 workshop were Christopher Arterton, Massachusetts Institute of Technology; Paul Allen Beck, University of Pittsburgh; Bruce D. Bowen, University of Michigan; C. Anthony Broh, Hobart & William Smith Colleges; Jere W. Bruner, Oberlin College; Donald A. Dixon, California State College, Sonoma; L. Douglas Dobson, Northern Illinois University; Ray A. Geigle, California State College, Bakersfield; Harlan Hahn, University of Southern California; Peter G. Hartjens, Franklin and Marshall College; Marvin K. Hoffman, Appalachian State University; Barry Hughes, Case Western Reserve University; Charles L. Prysby, University of North Carolina, Greensboro; John Paul Ryan, Vassar College and C. Neal Tate, North Texas State University. Workshop directors were William Buchanan, Washington and Lee University, and Betty A. Nesvold, San Diego State University. Sheilah Koeppen, Division of Educational Affairs, American Political Science Association, was the Project Director, and Lutz Erbring was the Director for the summer program of the Inter-University Consortium for Political Research.

This SETUPS, dealing with political socialization, gives students access to a unique set of data, interviews with parents and their children conducted in 1965 and the reinterviews with these same parents and children in 1973. The research was directed by M. Kent Jennings, Center for Political Studies, University of Michigan. The younger of the two related generations were high school seniors in 1965. Students using the SETUP formulate hypotheses about which of a series of political views (including party identification, presidential vote preference, cynicism, attitudes towards school integration, and political efficacy) are most likely and least likely to be transmitted from parents to children before the child leaves home. These hypotheses are tested using the 1965 data. Then the students formulate hypotheses about which of these political views are most likely and least likely to remain similar for parents and their children after the children have become adults. These hypotheses are tested using the 1973 reinterviews. More advanced exercises are provided which involve the student in analyses of parent and child change over this turbulent eight-year period and in the use of control variables. All but the advanced work can be done conveniently using percentages.

A "Note to the Instructor" in the Appendix provides suggestions for classroom use and deals with the computer aspects of the module.

William Buchanan
Editor

SETUPS: American Politics

The SETUPS in this series were designed for use in introductory classes in American Government. During the testing period they were widely used in these courses and were also found helpful in advanced classes. Data in the form of OSIRIS, SPSS or card image form for all SETUPS is provided by the Inter-University Consortium for Political Research, University of Michigan, without charge through an agreement with the American Political Science Association, for each order of 25 or more SETUPS.

SETUPS in the American Politics series are:

VOTING BEHAVIOR: The 1972 ELECTION by Bruce D. Bowen. C. Anthony Broh, Charles L. Prysby.
POLITICAL SOCIALIZATION ACROSS THE GENERATIONS by Paul Allen Beck, Jere W. Bruner, L. Douglas Dobson
POLITICAL PARTICIPATION by F. Christopher Arterton, Harlan Hahn
REPRESENTATION IN THE UNITED STATES CONGRESS: 1973 by Ray A. Geigle and Peter J. Hartjens
THE SUPREME COURT IN AMERICAN POLITICS: POLICY THROUGH LAW by John Paul Ryan, C. Neal Tate
U.S. ENERGY, ENVIRONMENT AND ECONOMIC PROBLEMS: A PUBLIC POLICY SIMULATION by Barry Hughes
THE DYNAMICS OF POLITICAL BUDGETING: A PUBLIC POLICY SIMULATION by Marvin K. Hoffman.

A second series of SETUPS, on topics in Comparative Politics, is being developed and tested in 1975-1976.

INTRODUCTION

Some Americans are Democrats, others are Republicans, and still others claim allegiance to no political party. Some are patriotic and exhibit their patriotism for all to see, while others are either less patriotic or more private in their demonstrations of patriotic feeling. Some dream of the integration of black and white school children, while others have nightmares about such integration. Some trust their government to do what is right most of the time, while others feel that government, when given a choice, will usually do what is wrong. Even on a recent political issue like the question of the impeachment of President Nixon, some Americans saw no evidence of the President's guilt and supported him to the end, while others saw convincing evidence of guilt and demanded his impeachment. The list of differences in the political views of American citizens is endless. At the same time, there are a number of political questions on which most Americans agree. Most feel loyalty to their nation and think that they should obey its laws. Most believe that democracy is a good form of government. Most believe that the government should see to it that the economy runs smoothly.

How do such political views develop? Why is there widespread agreement on some things but sharp disagreement on others? Students of politics have been deeply interested in answering these questions. In many cases, the answers have been sought in adult political experiences—such as political events, prevailing social or economic conditions, and interactions with friends and co-workers. Yet, since Plato and Aristotle, political thinkers have felt that the most important adult political orientations have their sources in childhood. Little attention was paid to the child's political world, though, until the late 1950s. At this time, several social scientists began to examine children's political orientations through the use of personal interviews with children themselves.[1] The work of these researchers has laid the foundation of an area of scholarly inquiry generally known as *political socialization*—an area which has grown and prospered in the subsequent years.

---

[1] The first two extensive interview studies of children's political views were conducted by Fred I. Greenstein in New Haven, Connecticut, and by researchers from the University of Chicago in predominantly white public schools within a number of large metropolitan areas. See the bibliography listings under Greenstein, Easton, and Hess for the major publications from these studies. Herbert Hyman, *Political Socialization* (New York: Free Press, 1959) summarizes political socialization research conducted prior to the late 1950s.

Political socialization research has uncovered a child's political world which is rich in content and in implications for adult political views. A rudimentary knowledge of government and politics appears as early as age seven, and this knowledge increases dramatically during the next few years.[2] The grade school years are also a time of strong attachment to the principal institutions and norms of American politics.[3] Nonetheless, there is ample evidence that this "rosy" view of politics can be affected by events such as the Watergate affair and by the location of some children outside of the mainstream of American life.[4] Another breach in the wall of consensus which generally characterizes young children's political views comes with the early development of attachments to a political party. As early as grade four, long before any grasp of political issues is gained, a majority of children have been found to think of themselves as either Democrats or Republicans.[5] Thus, one of the major sources of conflict among adults emerges very early in the life of the child.

Once the existence of a child's political world is established, the question of the sources of these political views becomes important. The primary *agent* of the child's political socialization seems to be the parents, though it is clear that children are rarely carbon copies of their parents.[6] The school (through its teachers and curriculum), other adults, the mass media, and other children show some evidence of being influential as well. An inquiry into the formation of children's political views, however, must begin with parents. Findings of previous research support the view that parental advantages in contact and their emotional ties with the child have a major impact. A number of interesting questions may be posed concerning the parental role in the political socialization process: What are the similarities and differences in the political views of parents and children? What kinds of political views are most likely to be passed on by parents to children? How durable are these inheritances as the child matures into an adult?

The following pages will focus primarily on these questions. You will be

[2] David Easton and Jack Dennis, "The Child's Image of Government," *The Annals of the American Academy of Political and Social Science,* 361 (September, 1965), pp. 40-57.

[3] *Ibid.,* and Fred I. Greenstein, *Children and Politics* (New Haven: Yale University Press, 1965), pp. 27-54.

[4] On Watergate, see F. Christopher Arterton, "The Impact of Watergate on Children's Attitudes toward Political Authority," *Political Science Quarterly,* 89 (June, 1974), pp. 269-283. On non-mainstream children, see Edward S. Greenberg (ed.), *Political Socialization* (New York: Atherton Press, 1970), pp. 85-190.

[5] Greenstein, *op. cit.,* pp. 71-75.

[6] Almost all major works on political socialization make this point. See especially James C. Davies, "The Family's Role in Political Socialization," *The Annals of the American Academy of Political and Social Science,* 361 (September, 1965), pp. 10-19; M. Kent Jennings and Richard G. Niemi, "The Transmission of Political Values from Parent to Child," *American Political Science Review,* 62 (March, 1968), pp. 169-184; and Robert E. Lane, "Fathers and Sons: Foundations of Political Belief," *American Sociological Review,* 24 (August, 1959), pp. 502-511. A dissenting view is registered in Robert D. Hess and Judith V. Torney, *The Development of Political Attitudes in Children* (Garden City, New York: Anchor Books, 1967), pp. 107-132.

asked to play a major part in providing answers to them by doing your own research. These are surely not the only important questions which are raised in the study of political socialization. Yet they are questions which bear considerable relevance to the study of politics, for answers to them can tell us a great deal about how the political views of the past are perpetuated in modern times and also about how political change takes place.

I. THE JENNINGS STUDY

The Interviews

A researcher at the University of Michigan's Center for Political Studies, Professor M. Kent Jennings, has gathered some data which allow us to study the political views of parents and their children in 1965 and then eight years later in 1973. In 1965, professionally-trained interviewers questioned at length a large number of high school seniors and their parents. The primary objective of the interview was to elicit detailed information on political and relevant non-political matters so that parent-child similarities and differences could be studied. For many of the seniors, 1965 was the last year of intimate day-to-day contact with their parents and, as a result, undoubtedly the end of a period in which their political learning could have come directly from their parents. After high school graduation, young people typically leave the parental home for college, the military, and their own home and family. Therefore, the senior year in high school is an excellent time to assess the effect that parents might have had in molding the political orientations of their children. Eight years later, in 1973, the Jennings research team reinterviewed these same *respondents* (this is the general term used to refer to those who answered the questions), repeating many of the questions asked in 1965.

The eight-year interval between interviews encompasses one of the most turbulent periods in American history. It was also a time during which those who were high school seniors in 1965 entered the adult world and encountered the new responsibilities of family, job, and political participation. Surely these two events—the turbulent 60s and maturation—have left a strong imprint on the political views of the younger generation. The Jennings data offer us the unparalleled opportunity to examine the durability of parental influence through this eight-year period. They also enable us to study persistence and change in the political orientations of the two generations separately. (See Part V for this emphasis.)

The result of the interviews is extensive information on the political views of over one thousand (1062 to be exact) related pairs of parents and children, members of two distinct generations, in two different years. Another feature of these data makes them even more valuable to students of political socialization. The 1062 pairs are not just any 1062 pairs. The high school seniors interviewed in 1965 were selected from almost one hundred schools, public and private, throughout the nation. They include blacks and whites; city dwellers, suburbanites, and people from small towns and rural areas; southerners, northerners, mid-westerners, and westerners; and poor, middle income, and rich. They were selected so that they represented all 1965 high school seniors and, by extension, all parents of 1965 high school seniors. The technique for representing a large number of people by a scientifically selected subset of the original group is called *sampling*. It is one of the most important tools employed by modern social scientists and, when done correctly, it has proven to be remarkably accurate.

Using the Codebook

The interviewers asked hundreds of questions in both 1965 and 1973. We have selected the questions which bear most directly on the process of political socialization for use here. At the end of this volume is a list of those questions, along with the numerical codes which represent their answers and other identifying information. Such a reference guide is called a *codebook.*

The codebook contains a great deal of information about the questions which are available to us, and it will be worthwhile to examine it in detail. Figure 1 contains a sample codebook entry—party identification for the younger generation in 1973. The pair of numbers in the upper left hand corner of this entry refers to the location of the party identification information on punched computer cards. The first number (1) is the deck number and the second number (3) is the column location in that deck for the party identification *variable*. (A *variable* is something which can assume different values. Party identification, for example, can be Democrat, Independent, or Republican.) Next, reading from left to right, is the identification number for this variable. Each question in the study yields at least one variable, and these variables are numbered sequentially beginning with 1. If you turn to the codebook at the end of this volume, you'll see for yourself that the variable numbers increase in order as we move from the first to the last variable on the list with only two exceptions. Because identifying information must be entered on each punched card, V73 and V74 are repeated at the end of deck two.

Immediately to the right of the variable's identification number is a short description of the variable—commonly called the variable name or variable label. Since most of the questions in the Jennings study were repeated four times, these descriptions have been prefixed by a code to identify the data source:

C65—child generation in 1965
C73—child generation in 1973
P65—parent generation in 1965
P73—parent generation in 1973

For example, C73 PARTY ID stands for the party identification of the younger generation in 1973. What do you think the variable description would be for the party identification of parents in the same year? (You may check your answer by consulting the description for variable V4 in the codebook.)

Below the variable description is the question asked in the interview and beneath it is the list of possible responses along with the numerical code assigned to each. This numerical code is the one that is keypunched onto a computer card when a respondent has given that answer. With party identification, for example, four different answers are possible. Democrat is coded as "1," Independent as "2," and Republican as "3." All other respondents were coded as "9," indicating that they did not answer the question. This is the code we shall use throughout to identify "missing data." Typically, missing data include answers such as "I don't know" or "I

Figure 1
Codebook Entry for Children's Party Identification, 1973

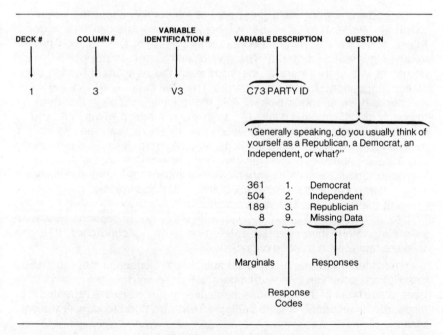

don't ever think about things like that" or even "I don't want to tell you about that." Missing data also include cases in which the question was

6

inappropriate—e.g., those who were not married would not, of course, be asked the party identification of their spouse. As a general rule, missing data should be eliminated in doing analysis, since they provide no usable information.

To the left of the numerical response code is another number—the actual number of individuals who gave that answer to the question and who are coded with that numerical code on the computer cards. For C73 PARTY ID, there were 361 Democrats, 504 Independents, 189 Republicans, and 8 respondents whose answers were classified as missing data. These numbers are generally referred to as marginal frequencies or just plain *marginals*. Since there are 1062 parent-child pairs in the Jennings study, the marginals in the codebook will always total 1062 when they are added and when missing data are included. If missing data are excluded, the total will usually be less than 1062.

The Political Orientations

The codebook entries describe each of the variables from the Jennings study which we shall examine. You should read through the codebook to familiarize yourself with them. Two different types of variables are included. On the one hand, there are a number of *political orientations*—ranging from preference for presidential candidate and party identification to general attitudes about government and politics. Our focus is on the transmission of these orientations from parents to their children and on changes in these orientations over time. We have included, however, a series of variables which might affect transmission and change in one way or another. (These are called "control" variables for reasons discussed in Part V.) Parental influence may be greater, for example, where parents are highly educated. Conversely, parental influence may be weakened by such post-adolescent experiences as marriage and college attendance. Certainly these experiences contribute to changes in the political views of the younger generation. The non-political variables (contained in Deck 2 of the codebook), will be examined in Part V. For the moment, we shall focus our attention on the political orientations.

Partisan Orientations. Two of the political variables, party identification (V1-V4) and presidential preference (V5-V8), measure the respondents' orientations to the major partisan objects on the political landscape—the political parties and those parties' candidates for President in the preceding year. Political scientists generally view party identification as an orientation which develops early in childhood and usually lasts throughout an individual's life. Party identifications seem to be passed on fairly successfully from parents to their children. Yet there seem to be times when this inheritance weakens as younger generations switch heavily to another party or to political independence.[7] What about you? Do you think

---

[7] Angus Campbell, Philip E. Converse, Warren E. Miller, and Donald E. Stokes, *The American Voter* (New York: Wiley and Sons, 1960), pp. 146-156.

that you have inherited a party identification from your parents? Or have the events of the past few years caused you to break away from the traditional party ties of your family?

Presidential preference refers to the respondent's preference in the preceding presidential election—the 1964 Johnson-Goldwater contest for the 1965 interviews and the 1972 McGovern-Nixon contest for the 1973 interviews. Unlike party identification, presidential preference is a political orientation with a relatively short life. The candidates for the Presidency usually change from one election to the next. Only the parties to which these candidates belong remain the same. Because of changing candidates from election to election, it seems doubtful that candidate preferences are orientations which are learned from parents during childhood and last throughout one's life. While parents probably influenced the high school seniors' preferences in 1964, such influence must surely weaken after the children leave the home. Whatever consistency there is between parents and their children in voting preference after the children have left the home should be due mainly to similarities in parent-child party identification and other views.

Political Ideology. Ideologies are commonly defined as systems of beliefs about the political world which are linked together by some overarching, abstract principle. If we stick to this definition, few Americans have political ideologies since few Americans think about politics consistently in abstract terms.[8] Words such as "conservative" and "liberal," though, have clear ideological content and are familiar to many Americans. You have probably used them yourself to describe parties or candidates. Respondents in the Jennings study were asked if they recognized these labels when attached to the political parties. That is, did they think of one party as more conservative than the other and, if yes, which party? While it stands to reason that these images of the political parties (V9-V12) are passed on from parents to children in many cases, it is equally plausible that these party images are based more on adult experiences than on childhood learning. Political socialization researchers have not studied this aspect of political ideology very much at all. It remains for you to utilize the Jennings data to examine the contribution of parents to the ideological thinking of the younger generation and to determine how stable these ideological images are over time.

Political ideologies may be involved even more directly in expressions of faith and confidence in particular levels of government. One of the central issues of ideological debate in the United States is the question of which level of government (national, state, or local) serves the people best. Democrats have believed for some time that the national government is best in this regard and that it should play an active role in solving our most pressing problems. On the other hand, Republicans have been distrustful of an active national government and have favored an upgrading of the role of

---

[8] *Ibid.,* pp. 188-215. For evidence on the absence of ideological thinking in children, see Greenstein, *op. cit.,* pp. 68-69.

the state and local governments in handling these problems. The respondents in the Jennings study were asked to take a position on this issue by indicating the level of government in which they had the most faith and confidence (V13-V16). Do these positions seem to you to be the sort that are likely to be passed on from parents to children? Or is it more likely that views as to which government is best depend upon how each level of government is performing at present or upon which party controls each level of government at a particular time?

Political Issues. Three other political variables represent the respondents' opinions on some of the important political issues of the day. One of these issues, school integration (V17-V20), has been in the forefront of public debate for quite some time and has generated strong feeling on both sides. Another issue which has aroused heated controversy is the question of whether prayers should be allowed in the public schools (V21-V24). A third issue involves the age-old question of tolerance of dissent. Respondents were asked if they thought speakers against churches and religion should be allowed to speak freely in their community (V110-V113) and whether a legally elected Communist should be allowed to take office (V114-V117). While neither of these specific issues has made newspaper headlines during the last decade, the general area to which they refer—tolerance of dissent—has been an important matter in an era of anti-Vietnam and pro-civil rights protest movements. Answers to these two questions were combined to yield a general measure of tolerance of dissent (V25-V28).

All three of these issues have undoubtedly been the subject of discussion in many homes and, as a result, we might expect parents to have passed on their views to children in a number of instances. At the same time, though, there has been a great deal of talk about the younger generation being more tolerant than their parents with regard to racial integration and dissent in particular.[9] Thus, as was the case with some of the preceding variables, there is some justification for expecting *either* high parent-child agreement on these matters *or* a younger generation which is quite different from its parents. What would you expect for these political issues?

These are the only political issues contained in both the 1965 and the 1973 interviews. Absent are questions about the war in Vietnam, the energy crisis, the environment, inflation and recession, the "Watergate affair," and a host of other issues which have moved to political center stage since 1965. The reason for their absence is simple. They were not important issues in 1965. Even the war in Vietnam generated little interest among high school seniors and their parents at that time.

Political Cynicism. The level of cynicism at which citizens respond to their

---

[9] On the socialization of racial attitudes, see Herbert Hyman, "Social Psychology and Race Relations," in Irwin Katz and Patricia Gurin. (eds.), *Race and the Social Sciences* (New York: Basic Books, 1969), pp. 6-9. On tolerance generally, see Samuel A. Stouffer, *Communism, Conformity, and Civil Liberties* (Gloucester, Massachusetts: Peter Smith, 1963), pp. 89-108.

political leaders and government is a fundamental orientation towards politics. A democratic system of government is predicated upon public confidence that leaders are capable and just. Surely if a large number of people feel that politicians are crooked and stupid, and that government wastes money, rarely does what is right, and operates in favor of a few big interests, no political system, democratic or otherwise, can function smoothly.

The level of cynicism about American government and politics has increased dramatically in recent years.[10] Perhaps this comes as no surprise to you, if you have become more cynical as well. One can easily point to reasons why people might have soured on their government and its leaders—the "credibility gap" over Vietnam, the Watergate affair, the illegal CIA and FBI activities, and the difficulties government has had in solving our most pressing economic and social problems. Yet, some observers contend that the *exposure* of corruption and illegality in government is a healthy sign for American democracy and that no government has a better record than ours in solving today's complex problems. To these observers, recent increases in cynicism seem unwarranted and should soon be reversed due to corrective mechanisms in the system itself.

The Jennings study allows us to examine changes in cynicism among parents and their children between 1965 to 1973—a period when Americans in general were becoming much more cynical. Previous socialization research would lead us to expect the younger generation to become more cynical merely as a result of passage from the idealistic political world of children to the adult political world.[11] But the increases in cynicism which have been recorded in the United States during the past few years suggest that much more is happening than the maturation of younger generations. The roots of cynicism may well lie in the political events of the past decade. What do you think? How would you explain the dramatic increases in cynicism among Americans?

The Jennings study contains five different questions which assay political cynicism: Do people in government waste the money we pay in taxes (V29-V32)? Can you trust the government in Washington to do what is right (V33-V36)? How many of the people who run the government are crooked (V37-V40)? Do the people running the government know what they are doing (V41-V44)? Is the government run by a few big interests looking out for themselves or in the interest of all the people (V45-V48)? These questions should be familiar to you, for they are questions many of us may have raised in our own minds. Because each of the questions seems interesting in its own right, we have included all of them for you to examine. We have also included a total cynicism score—a simple measure of

---

[10] See in particular, Arthur H. Miller, "Political Issues and Trust in Government," *American Political Science Review,* 68 (September, 1974), pp. 951-972, and the "Comment" and "Rejoinder" which follow it.

[11] Robert D. Hess and Judith V. Torney, *Op. Cit.,* pp. 39-68.

cynicism (V49-V52) which combines the answers to all five individual questions so that the most cynical respondents receive the highest score.

Political Interest. As you well know, people differ substantially in their interest in politics—or rock music, sports, etc. Respondents in the Jennings study were asked how interested they were in politics (V53-V56). It seems likely that parental interest in politics contributes a good deal to the interests of children. Thus, one should expect a fair amount of similarity in the interest levels of parents and their children. Yet, there are also reasons (such as the greater relative education of the younger generation or the unusually turbulent nature of politics in recent years) to expect that the children will come to pay more attention to politics by their mid-20s than their parents do. What do you think? Will the younger generation be more or less interested in politics by 1973 than the parental generation?

Respondents were also asked to indicate the relative amount of attention they paid to each of four types of political affairs—international, national, state, and local. Those who ranked international and national politics ahead of state and local may be called "cosmopolitans" because their interests are broader. Those who ranked state and local politics ahead of international and national may be called "locals." The variable (V57-V60) itself is called LOCALISM, since those with the highest scores have ranked state and local politics the highest. These orientations may be passed on from parents to children like the other orientations we have examined. It also seems likely that interest in the more local spheres would grow as the individual comes into closer contact with the things local governments do—provision of education, police protection, trash collection, etc. Thus, among the middle aged, particularly those with their own houses and children, localism might be more prevalent.

Political Knowledge. A possible companion of political interest is knowledge about politics (V61-V64). It stands to reason that those who are more interested in politics would know more about it. The importance of education and intelligence, though, should not be ignored in accounting for the amount of knowledge a person has about anything. All respondents in the Jennings study were given a political knowledge test comprised of the following six questions: To what party did Franklin Roosevelt belong? Of what nation is Marshall Tito the leader? How many members are there on the United States Supreme Court? Who is the governor of your state? Which nation had a great many concentration camps for Jews during World War II? How many years does a United States Senator serve? (How did you do on this test? You can compare your test score with those of the parents and the students by consulting the codebook marginal frequencies.)

Since parents probably do not drill the answers to such questions into the heads of their children it seems unlikely that we would find much transmission of political knowledge from parent to child. Intelligence is passed on through inheritance, however, and parents and their children might obtain similar test scores even though no direct transmission of orientations has occurred. Do you think that a similar problem of separating actual transmission from coincidental agreement might occur for some of the other political orientations?

Political Influence. One of the basic concerns of political scientists in studying political systems is the degree of influence people can exert on their leaders. Democracies are supposed to accord the individual more opportunities for influence than non-democracies, but no one assumes that all citizens are influential even in a democracy. Respondents were asked to estimate their political influence by responding to two different questions: Is voting the only way people can have any say about how the government runs things? Are politics and government so complicated that sometimes a person can not really understand what is going on? Those who answered "no" to both questions thought themselves to be politically influential or, as political scientists say, politically efficacious. Those who answered in the opposite fashion are inefficacious. The political efficacy variable (V65-V68) we shall use scores the most efficacious respondents the highest and the least efficacious the lowest.

Political efficacy is another orientation which seems likely to have been passed on from parent to child. After all, children typically have no experience in attempting to influence government. On the other hand, many parents have made such attempts at some time in their lives.[12] Where the attempts were successful, the parents may rightly feel efficacious. Where they were not, a sense of inefficacy seems justified. Such feelings, with their sources deeply embedded in political experience, may well color parental discussions of politics and, as a result, help shape the children's views. It is a fundamental fact of political life in this nation (and all nations), however, that even parental experience in influencing government is limited. This leaves room for more general views of the citizen's role in government, such as political cynicism, to influence children's orientations. It also leaves room for children's quasi-political experiences in decision making in the home or school to affect their feelings of political efficacy.[13]

This exhausts the list of political variables contained in the codebook. As you might have guessed, Jennings asked the respondents many more politically-relevant questions than the ones we have included. The ones we have chosen seem to us to be the most interesting as well as the ones most useful to you in developing an understanding of the process of political socialization. These variables are valuable in another way: they were the ones which were measured for both children and parents in 1965 and in 1973.

---

[12] Verba and Nie estimate that over three-quarters of all American citizens have attempted to influence government in some fashion. About one-fourth limited their attempts to voting, but over half of all citizens participated in a manner beyond voting. Nonetheless, very few Americans come close to the democratic ideal of the political activist. See Sidney Verba and Norman H. Nie, *Participation in America* (New York: Harper and Row, 1972), pp. 79-80.

[13] The impact of participation in family and school decision-making processes on political efficacy is shown in Gabriel Almond and Sidney Verba, *The Civic Culture* (Princeton, New Jersey: Princeton University Press, 1963), pp. 328-374.

II. THE POLITICAL VIEWS OF TWO GENERATIONS THROUGH TIME

Interpreting the Marginals

The marginal frequencies for each of the variables are presented in the codebook. These marginals tell us how the political and non-political variables are distributed for the parent and child generations in both 1965 and 1973. Comparing the marginal frequencies for different groups and different questions often proves difficult, however, because frequencies are meaningful only when you know the size of the total group. For instance, if you were to tell a friend that there are 361 Democrats among the younger generation in the Jennings study in 1973, your friend would want to know how many members of this generation were included in the study. You could convey both pieces of information in a single number by telling your friend instead that 34 percent of this generation called themselves Democrats in 1973.

Percentages express a category frequency relative to the total number of respondents and, as a consequence, simplify greatly our task of comparison. They are computed from the marginal frequencies by dividing the number in each response category by the total number of respondents and then multiplying by 100 to move the decimal points. Taking the party identification variable for the younger generation in 1973, for example, we have:

Democrats = 361/1062 = .340 x 100 = 34.0%
Independents = 504/1062 = .475 x 100 = 47.5%
Republicans = 189/1062 = .178 x 100 = 17.8%
Missing Data = 8/1062 = .008 x 100 = 0.8%

The percentages for each of the sub-groups should add to 100.0%. In some cases, however, they will deviate slightly from this total due to the rounding off of trailing digits. The computations presented above represent one of these cases: the total is 100.1%.

For many purposes, the percentages based on the number of respondents who answered the question are more appropriate than the percentages based on all respondents. That is, missing data are often eliminated from the total on which the percentage is based. Doing this for party identification of the younger generation in 1973 yields:

Democrats $= 361/1054 = .343 \times 100 = 34.3\%$
Independents $= 504/1054 = .478 \times 100 = 47.8\%$
Republicans $= 189/1054 = .179 \times 100 = 17.9\%$

Parent and Child Party Identifications in 1973

We know from another study of party identification that a sample representing the entire American electorate had the following distribution of party loyalties in 1973:[14]

Democrats $= 36\%$
Independents $= 41\%$
Republicans $= 21\%$
Missing Data $= 2\%$

These figures differ from those we have just examined for the younger generation in the Jennings study during the same year. The younger generation is more Independent and less Democratic or Republican (or, we can simply say less "partisan") than the electorate as a whole. These differences would be expected by political scientists. In the past twenty years, they have found that younger voters as a group are more Independent and less partisan than their elders.[15] Yet while parties are less important for the 1973 younger voters on the whole, the Democratic party is far more popular than the Republican party among partisans.

Exercise No. 1: 1973 Party Identification for the Two Generations

1. Would you expect the parent generation to be more or less Independent than the younger generation? Would you expect the Democratic party to be more or less favored among partisans in the parent generation than among partisans in the younger generation?
2. Why do you expect this?
3. Test your expectations by calculating and then interpreting the following from the appropriate codebook marginals:
   (a) the percentage of Independents in the parent generation (the parallel percentage for the children was presented in the text); and
   (b) the percentage of Democrats *among partisans* for both the parent and child generations.
4. Were your expectations fulfilled? Explain why or why not. If not, how would you modify your expectations to make them more accurate the next time?
5. Think about your results. What do they suggest might happen to the two political parties in the future?

---

[14] This survey was conducted in November, 1973, by the Center for Political Studies at the University of Michigan.

[15] Campbell *et al., op. cit.*, pp. 161-162.

In completing Exercise No. 1, you have done the same things that all researchers do when they study a problem. First you have formulated what is called an *hypothesis.* An hypothesis is really nothing more than an expectation about what the results should look like. Your hypotheses or expectations should be based on the best information you have about the matter under study. That is why political scientists, and all scientists for that matter, pay particular attention to what others who have studied the same problem or question have found. Your hypotheses should also be the result of a great deal of careful thought. In other words, it is not enough to say "I expect to find such and such." You must also provide reasonable justifications for your expectations.

Often several different expectations can be justified. Even scientists working on the same problem may disagree on what hypotheses seem to be the most plausible. In our discussion of some of the political variables, we outlined alternative expectations about the relationship between parents and their children. For example, we contended that tolerance of dissent may be a political orientation which is passed on intact from parents to children or that it may be generally higher among the younger generation, and, thus, less consonant with parental views. Stating alternatives such as these is often quite useful in our thinking—principally because it forces us to justify our expectations. This justification is an important step in political inquiry.

This takes us to the second step engaged in by researchers—they test their hypotheses in the real world. If your hypothesis is that young adults today are more Republican than their parents, you would not want to stop there. You would want to go on to show that the expectation was correct, and you might do so by comparing members of the two generations. Of course, your answer would be influenced by which members you selected to represent the two generations. If you chose members of the Young Republican Club in your school to represent the younger generation, you might find that a few of their parents were Democrats and then conclude that the young were more Republican than their parents. But this would hardly be a statement which could apply equally well to the entire generation. In other words, before you would be satisfied that you had tested your hypothesis adequately, you would want to examine groups representative of the child and parent generations—not a special group such as the Young Republicans. Once the expectations or hypotheses are tested with representative data, the hypotheses may be either confirmed or discarded, and we have learned something about politics in either case.

The Changing Political Views of Parent and Child Generations

So far we have compared only pairs of marginals in a single year. While these comparisons provide us with some interesting information, the Jennings data allow us to answer other interesting questions as well. To what extent is each generation changing over time? Are the children, as they enter adulthood, becoming more or less like their parents? To answer

15

these questions, we must compare four sets of marginals—one for each generation in both 1965 and 1973. As you can imagine, such a comparison would become quite complicated unless a method was devised to handle the four pieces of data simultaneously. In his initial report on the 1973 study, Jennings presented such a method.[16] The percentage with a particular response is compared for each generation in 1965 and 1973 by simply graphing the over-time change of parents and children separately. The method ignores other responses in order to portray change as clearly as possible.

Figure 2 shows the result of applying the Jennings method to the party identification question. The percentages of Independents for the parents and children at each time point have been entered on the graph and can be compared quite readily. It is apparent from this figure that parents have remained the same with respect to the percentage of Independents while the children have changed substantially. This is what political scientists would expect. People are supposed to be less stable in partisanship when they are young. It is likewise apparent that the child generation has become *more Independent* over time. This is not what political scientists would normally expect! Rather, in previous eras, people have become more partisan as they grew older.[17] It is clear from these data that the hypothesis that partisanship *always* increases with age must be rejected. Perhaps there is something about modern times which defies the old regularities of behavior, or perhaps these regularities do not hold for the age span of 18 to 26. Whatever the explanation for this phenomenon, it is clear that a "generation gap" exists in party identification which is widening rather than narrowing.

This finding of generational differences in partisanship between the parents and the children in the Jennings study may be set into a broader context. Since 1964, the percentage of Independents in the American electorate has increased substantially, while the percentages of Democrats and Republicans have both declined. What we have learned in our analysis, if we think about it for a moment, may suggest why this happened. The parents exhibited virtually no net change between 1965 and 1973, but the political independence of the younger generation *grew*. This implies that recent changes in the partisanship of the American electorate owe to the replacement of older voters,[18] as they die off, by much less partisan generations of younger voters. If this generational replacement process continues, the Democratic and Republican parties may become less important parts of the American scene.

---

[16] M. Kent Jennings and Richard G. Niemi, "Continuity and Change in Political Orientations: A Longitudinal Study of Two Generations," *American Political Science Review*, 69 (September, 1975).

[17] Campbell *et al., op. cit.,* pp. 161-162.

[18] This interpretation is documented in Paul Allen Beck, "A Socialization Theory of Partisan Realignment," in Richard G. Niemi and Associates, *The Politics of Future Citizens* (San Francisco: Jossey-Bass, 1974), pp. 199-219.

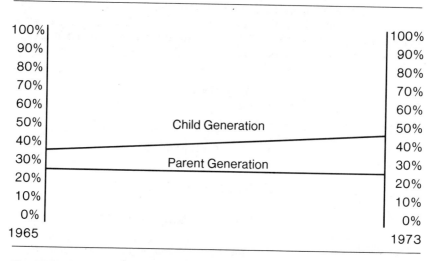

Figure 2
Parent and Child Independents, 1965 and 1973

100%	100%
90%	90%
80%	80%
70%	70%
60%	60%
50%	Child Generation	50%
40%	40%
30%	Parent Generation	30%
20%	20%
10%	10%
0%	0%
1965	1973

Exercise No. 2: Comparing Generations Over Time
1. Select two different political orientations from the codebook. The first should be one for which you expect the child and the parent generations to become more similar in their views between 1965 and 1973. The second should be one for which you expect these generations to retain their differences or even increase them during this time. (Review the preceding section on political orientations before formulating your expectations or hypotheses.)
2. Why do you expect the variables you have selected to exhibit these characteristics?
3. Test your hypotheses by entering the marginal percentages in the appropriate places in a chart like that in Figure 2.
4. Were your hypotheses supported? Explain why or why not. If not, how would you modify them to make them more accurate the next time?

For some of the variables you could have selected in Exercise No. 2, the two generations become more similar in their political views over the eight-year time interval, as the younger generation changes. Panel A of Figure 3 is an example of such a convergence. This is a pattern characteristic of what are called *life cycle effects*. That is to say, it is a pattern which we might find if the contrasting viewpoints of the two generations are the result of their different ages (or their different stages in the cycle of life) and are not set for a lifetime. If we were to compare parents and their children at the same age, we would expect to find no differences if only life cycle effects were operating.

For other variables you might have selected, the two generations have remained as far apart or have moved even farther apart over the time period. This pattern, shown in Panel B of Figure 3, is characteristic of what is called a *generational effect*. That is, the two generations have contrasting views which seem likely to be retained throughout their lives.

Figure 3
Life Cycle, Generational, and Period Effects

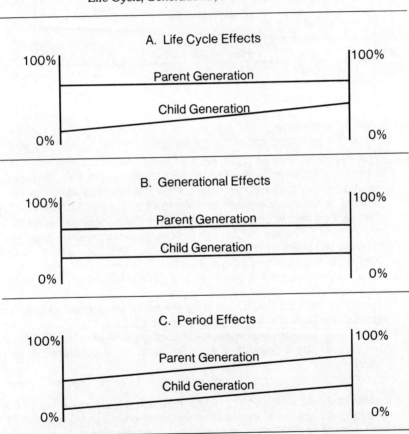

The life cycle and generational patterns may be complicated by the effects on both generations of the extraordinary political events between 1965 and 1973. For many of the variables, both generations recorded substantial change over this time period. This simultaneous change, termed *period effects* since it reflects responses to the politics of the period, is depicted in Panel C of Figure 3. Of course, the three patterns presented in Figure 3 represent only some of the patterns which may appear. Any two, or even all three, of the effects may appear together. For example, Panel 3 contains both period and generational effects—though both generations change, the gap between them remains the same.

Now that labels have been assigned to the three types of change which may be reflected in your figures, you should return to Exercise No. 2 and apply the labels to what you have found. This may not be easy to do, because reality often combines several types of change. The party identification data presented in Figure 2, in fact, are more easily interpreted than most. They show increasing generational differences over time and little hint of the usual life cycle changes in partisanship. But, even here, the very absence of expected patterns of change suggests that period effects are at work.

Conclusion

You have now been introduced to the Jennings study—the data which will be the focus of our discussion and your analysis in the following pages. The marginals for these data, as you have seen, contain a great deal of interesting information about the two generations in the aggregate. The marginals, though, do not enable us to examine the political socialization process directly. While we might expect that the similarities in the marginals result from the family ties between the parent and child pairs, we need to examine the pairs directly to subject this expectation to real world testing. That is, we need to determine the degree of similarity in the political views of parents and their children. It is to this task that we shall now turn.

III. THE TRANSMISSION OF PARENTAL POLITICAL VIEWS

Introduction

In the preceding section, we examined a number of important political orientations. We discussed, for example, the nature of party identification and examined its distribution (i.e., the marginals) among parents and children in both 1965 and 1973. In completing Exercises 1 and 2, you examined the distributions of one or two other important political variables. Finally, we have introduced the notions of generational, period, and life cycle effects in order to account for patterns of divergence, simultaneous change, and convergence between parents and children over the eight years.

The examples and exercises of Part II, however, do not answer a most important question about political socialization: from where do political attitudes and opinions come? This question is so important that many scholars have devoted years of their lives to the search for an answer. In general, these scholars have argued that political views have their roots in the influence of several different agents of political socialization—family, school, peer groups, and even the mass media. The most important of these agents is commonly thought to be the family. Among family members, parents are usually seen as playing the dominant role in socializing children.

There are good reasons for an emphasis on the role of parents in the socialization process. If you were to think about your own experiences for a moment, you would probably reach a similar conclusion. With whom did you most frequently interact as a child? Who rewarded you for saying the "right" things and punished you for saying the "wrong" things? When you were a child, whom did you most admire and want to be like? While there are certainly some exceptions, most of you probably answered "mother," "father," or "my parents" to each of these questions. If this is true, it seems logical that many of us would turn out to share our parents' political views.

There are equally good reasons, of course, why children might not turn out to view politics exactly as their parents do on every issue. For example, college students whose parents do not have a college education may have views of the political world quite different from those of their parents. Furthermore, political disagreement between a child's mother and father

21

force the child to disagree with at least one of them. We should not be surprised if children do not always turn out to be carbon copies of their parents. Rather, we may expect some children to share the political views of their parents and others to disagree. The interesting questions here concern the relative number of the former compared to the latter, and the reasons for agreement or disagreement.

Constructing Crosstab Tables

In the exercises of Part II, the marginal frequencies for several variables were examined. In the text, an extended example was provided which analyzed the marginals for party identification. If we continue our use of party identification, but this time look at 1965 instead of 1973, we have:

Among children in 1965

425 identified with the Democratic party
387 identified as Independents
239 identified with the Republican party

Among parents in 1965

481 identified with the Democratic party
271 identified as Independents
294 identified with the Republican party

These data tell us about the party attachments of two groups of individuals—parents and children—and about how similar the two groups are. But if we wish to understand fully the role of parents in the socialization process, it is not enough to know only that parents as a group are, or are not, similar to children as a group. Rather, we must know whether *individual* parents are, or are not, similar to their children. To do that in the case of party identification, we need a way to match each child's party identification to that of his or her parent. We must show how many Democratic parents had Democratic, Independent, or Republican children; how many Independent parents had Democratic, Independent, or Republican children; and how many Republican parents had Democratic, Independent, or Republican children.

In order to accomplish this, one might build a table which looks like Table 1.

You can think of the boxes (they are frequently called "*cells*") in the table as nine boxes into which marbles are going to be dropped. Each marble represents a parent-child pair. The instructions that would allow you to construct the table would read something like this:

List each parent's party identification beside his or her child's party identification. If the parent is a Democrat and the child is a Democrat, drop a marble into the box in the first row and first column. (A row goes across the page; a column goes down the page.) If the parent is a Democrat and the child is an Independent, drop a marble into the box in the sec-

22

Table 1

Comparing Parents and Their Children

| | | Parent 1965 Party Identification | | | |
		Democrat	Independent	Republican	
Child 1965 Party Identification	Democrat	number of Democratic parents with Democratic children	number of Independent parents with Democratic children	number of Republican parents with Democratic children	Total number of Democratic children
	Independent	number of Democratic parents with Independent children	number of Independent parents with Independent children	number of Republican parents with Independent children	Total number of Independent children
	Republican	number of Democratic parents with Republican children	number of Independent parents with Republican children	number of Republican parents with Republican children	Total number of Republican children
		Total number of Democratic parents	Total number of Independent parents	Total number of Republican parents	Total number of parent and child pairs

ond row and the first column. If the parent is a Democrat and the child is a Republican, drop a marble into the box in the third row and the first column. Proceed in a like manner for Independent parents (second column) and Republican parents (third column). When you have finished comparing the party identifications of all parents and children, count the number of marbles in each box and note it on a form similar to the one above.

This operation—whether it is done by hand or with a computer—results in a *cross-tabulation* (crosstab) of parent and child 1965 party identifications. Adding the numbers across each of the rows in this crosstab table will produce the marginal frequencies for the party identification of children in 1965. Similarly, adding the numbers down each of the columns will produce

23

the marginal frequencies for parent party identification in 1965. You should also notice that this table excludes people who did not answer the question about their party identification (i.e., missing data). We will eliminate such missing data throughout the remainder of this volume. While it is very important, for some purposes, to study the kinds of people who do not answer questions, that is not our main purpose here.

Having constructed this kind of table, we are ready to answer a range of interesting questions about the similarity of parent and child party identifications. We will turn to those questions after you have completed Exercise 3.

Exercise No. 3: Constructing a Crosstab Table from Data

Suppose that we have a sample of 50 parents and their children. We first ask each child to indicate his or her party preference. We next ask each parent to indicate his or her party preference. We record a "1" if the answer is Democratic, a "2" if the answer is Independent, and a "3" if the answer is Republican. When we have finished questioning all of the children and parents our data look like this.

Pair number	Child Party ID	Parent Party ID
1	1	1
2	2	1
3	1	1
4	1	2
5	2	3
6	3	1
7	2	2
8	2	2
9	1	1
10	1	1
11	1	1
12	1	3
13	3	2
14	3	3
15	3	3
16	3	3
17	1	3
18	2	3
19	2	2
20	2	2
21	1	2
22	3	1
23	1	1
24	1	1
25	2	1
26	2	1
27	2	3

24

28	3	3
29	3	3
30	1	2
31	1	1
32	1	1
33	1	1
34	2	2
35	2	2
36	1	3
37	1	2
38	1	3
39	2	3
40	2	3
41	2	1
42	1	1
43	1	1
44	3	3
45	2	1
46	2	2
47	2	2
48	3	2
49	3	3
50	3	3

1. Using these data, construct a crosstab table for parent and child party identifications.
2. Using your table, answer the following questions.
   a. How many of the children are Democrats? (If your answer is not 20, you should try to construct the table again.)
   How many of the children are Independents? How many of the children are Republicans?
   b. How many Democratic parents have Democratic children?
   How many Republican parents have Independent children?
   How many Independent parents have Democratic children?
   c. What is the total number of children and parents with the same party affiliation? With different party affiliations?
   d. What is the percentage of parents and children with the same party affiliation? With different party affiliations?

Parent-Child Agreement on Political Orientations

Now that you have an understanding of how crosstab tables are constructed, let us return to a consideration of party identification in the Jennings data. Think, for just a moment, about your own experience. If someone had asked you, during your senior year of high school, whether you called yourself a Democrat, an Independent, or a Republican, what would you have said? Would you have chosen the same party that your parents would have chosen? How about your closest friends? Would they have chosen the same political party as their parents? Thinking about your own experience and the experiences of your closest friends, how many of the children and parents inverviewed in the Jennings study would you expect to have chosen the political party of their parents—all, most, some, or very few?

Now you have a hypothesis about political socialization, but hypotheses are not very useful unless we can test them. Let us take the 1965 party identification of children and the 1965 party identification of parents and build a crosstab table. This will tell us the number of children who prefer the Democratic party, the Republican party, or are Independents (that is, it will give us the marginals for 1965 children). It will also tell us the number of parents who prefer the Democratic party, the Republican party, or are Independents (the 1965 parent marginals). But, more importantly, it will provide a count of the number of times each of the following occurs: (1) parent is a Democrat and child is (a) a Democrat, (b) an Independent, (c) a Republican; (2) parent is an Independent and child is (a) a Democrat, (b) an Independent, (c) a Republican; (3) parent is a Republican and child is (a) a Democrat, (b) an Independent, (c) a Republican. Now, if we add up the counts for 1a, 2b, and 3c, we can determine how many parents and children are in agreement. Similarly, we can calculate the number of parents and children who disagree by adding the counts in the remaining cells.

The data on 1965 party identification taken from the Jennings study are presented in Table 2 below.[19]

Table 2

Frequencies for Parent-Child Party Identification in 1965

| | | Parent | | | |
		Democrat	Independent	Republican	Total
	Democrat	306	79	33	418
Child	Independent	136	137	108	381
	Republican	37	49	151	237
		479	265	292	1036

By adding the numbers in the agreement cells, you will find that 594 of the parent-child pairs were in agreement on their party attachment in 1965. This leaves 442 student-parent pairs who selected different parties in

---

[19] Note that only 1036 of the 1062 parent-child pairs are included in this table. Absences are due to missing data on party identification for either the parent or the child—or both.

1965. Was your hypothesis correct? Can you think of any reasons why 442 of the parent-child pairs might have chosen different parties? (What about families where one parent belongs to one party and the other parent belongs to another, for example? Are there other reasons that you can think of?)

It is often awkward to deal with raw numbers in tables, and their meaning is not always obvious. Social scientists almost always convert the numbers into percentages. There are two useful ways to calculate percentages for this table. Each way answers a slightly different question. The first way is to calculate what are called *total-percentages*. These are percentages whose base is the number of parent-child pairs in the entire table. Table 3 below gives total-percentages for party identification.[20]

Table 3

Total-Percentages for Parent-Child Party Identification in 1965

		Parent			
		Democrat	Independent	Republican	Total
	Democrat	29.5	7.6	3.2	40.3
Child	Independent	13.1	13.2	10.4	36.7
	Republican	3.6	4.7	14.6	22.9
		46.2	25.5	28.2	100.0

The percentages in this table were calculated by dividing the total number of parent-child pairs into the number of parent-child pairs in each of the cells and multiplying the result by 100. Thus the cell that is in row one and column one at the upper left is given by (306/1036) x 100 = 29.5. The multiplication by 100 simply converts proportions to percentages. Likewise the cell entry in row three, column three is given by (151/1036) x 100 = 14.6. The marginal percentages are calculated in exactly the same way that you calculated them in Part II—that is, by dividing the number of cases in each of the categories by the total number of cases and multiplying by 100.

If you wanted to know how many of the parents and children in the sample "agreed" —that is, had the same party identification—what would you do? One reasonable procedure would be to add the total-percentages of Democratic parents-Democratic children, Independent parents-Independent children, and Republican parents-Republican children. This would give

---

[20] Due to the rounding of trailing digits, these percentages do not quite add to 100.0.

the total-percentage of parent-child pairs that agreed on party identification. This is, in fact, the approach that we will take in showing the extent of agreement in what follows. There are, of course, other ways to measure parent-child agreement, as we will explain later. But this one will do for now.

When we calculate agreement in this way, it will be called the *percent agreement measure*. In a table such as the one above with three rows and three columns, the percent agreement measure will always be calculated by adding the percentages in row one-column one, row two-column two, and row three-column three. In Table 3 you can see that the percent agreement is 57.3 (i.e., 29.5 + 13.2 + 14.6). Thus, 57.3 percent of all parent-child pairs had the same identification with a political party in 1965. By adding the percentages in the remaining cells, we can also calculate the percent disagreement. For Table 3 the percent disagreement is 42.6.

Differential Transmission of Political Orientations from Parents to Children

Suppose that we are now interested in the extent to which different groups of parents have children who share their political orientations. In particular, what if we wanted to know how likely it was that Democratic parents would have Democratic children; that Independent parents would have Independent children; and that Republican parents would have Republican children? In that case we would have to calculate, for Democratic parents, the percentage of Democratic, Independent, or Republican children; for Independent parents, the percentage of Democratic, Independent, or Republican children; and finally, for Republican parents, the percentage of Democratic, Independent, or Republican children. In other words, we would calculate percentages in each column of the cross-tabulation table.

The *column-percentages* for party identification are shown in Table 4. In this table, we have calculated the number in each cell as a percentage of the total number of cases in each column. Therefore, the percentage in row one and column one is given by (306/479) x 100 = 63.9. You should notice that the percentages in each column sum to 100 percent or very close to it.

What does this table tell us about political socialization? The first thing to notice is that a majority of high school seniors in 1965 had the same party identification as their parents in each category. Looking at the first column, you will find that of those parents who called themselves Democrats in 1965, 63.9 percent had children who also called themselves Democrats. Looking in the second column, of the Independent parents, 51.7 percent had children who called themselves Independents. Finally, in the third column, 51.7 percent of the Republican parents had children who called themselves Republicans.

Three other points emerge from a careful examination of this table. First, Democratic parents seem to have had greater success in transmitting party

Table 4

Column-Percentages for Parent-Child Party Identification in 1965

		Parent			
		Democrat	Independent	Republican	Total
	Democrat	63.9	29.8	11.3	40.3
Child	Independent	28.4	51.7	37.0	36.8
	Republican	7.7	18.5	51.7	22.9
		100.0	100.0	100.0	100.0
		(479)	(265)	(292)	(1036)

attachments than either Independent or Republican parents. While 51.7 percent of the children of both Independent and Republican parents had the same party identification as their parents, 63.9 percent of the children of Democratic parents had the same party identification as their parents. Second, 1965 seniors who did not adopt the party of their parents did not often identify with the opposite party. Rather, they tended to be Independents. While 28.4 percent of the children with Democratic parents said that they were Independents, only 7.7 percent said that they were Republicans. If you look at the Republican parents column, you will see that similar results are obtained for children of Republican parents. The final point concerns the Independent parents column. The question that we have in mind is this: "What party were the children of Independent parents most likely to identify with when they did not agree with their parents?" If you look at the Independent parent column, the answer is clear. The Democratic party had a clear advantage in 1965: 29.8 percent of the children with Independent parents identified themselves as Democrats while only 18.5 percent identified themselves as Republicans.

If we take a moment to reflect on the results of our analysis of Tables 3 and 4, we might reach something like the following conclusion: "On the whole, it seems that 1965 parents were fairly successful in passing their basic partisan attachments along to their children. After all, over half of the high school seniors identified with the same party as their parents. Moreover, Democratic parents seem to have been more successful in transmitting party affiliation than either Independent or Republican parents." The data certainly seem to support such an assertion. But one must be very careful in drawing conclusions from data such as these for several reasons.

First, consider what is meant by the notion of "success" in transmitting political orientations from parents to children. At what point should we decide that the socialization process is successful? When 30 percent of children have the same views as their parents? When 70 percent do? Or, shall we require that all children have the same views as their parents before we conclude that socialization is operating successfully? The answer to these questions depends, essentially, upon our expectations about the potency of parental influence. Socialization researchers would base their expectations on the findings of previous research and observation. Prior to the Jennings study, very few extensive studies of the impact of parents had been conducted. As a result, the expectations of researchers varied considerably. Your experience, while probably less extensive and less systematic than social science research, will undoubtedly serve as the source of your expectations. Since no two people share exactly the same experience, different expectations should emerge from the class. In short, there is no easy answer to the question of the meaning of success in absolute terms.

It is far easier to answer a question about the *relative* success of parents across different opinion areas. In raising this kind of question, we are making an effort to identify and classify those political orientations which seem to be passed on more or less successfully from generation to generation. Perhaps your intuition suggests, as ours does, that different beliefs, opinions, and values will show widely divergent rates of agreement between parents and their children. For something as basic as religious preference, for example, we might expect much higher levels of parent-child agreement than we found for party identification. As a matter of fact, this turns out to have been true in 1965. Over 93 percent of the parent-child pairs in the Jennings data fell into the same general category of religious denomination. In other areas, one might expect the level of parent-child agreement to be lower than that found for 1965 party identification. For example although there are no data in the Jennings study on attitudes towards the legalization of marijuana in 1965, this political issue might be one where we would expect to find relatively low levels of correspondence between parents and children.

A second problem which underlies attempts to draw strong conclusions about socialization relates to the consistency with which parents hold particular views over time. This problem is a complex one, and we do not intend to fully treat it here. Your intuition about the difficulties involved will develop as you work through the next two chapters. But to illustrate the point, consider the views discussed above—religious preference, party identification, and opinion on marijuana legalization—from the perspective of parents. We might expect that religious preference would be highly stable for parents. That is, individuals who prefer Catholic, Protestant, or Jewish faiths tend to remain in that faith and do not readily change. On the question of party identification, this kind of expectation is somewhat less realistic, but we might still expect many people to develop relatively long-term attachments to one or another of the political parties. On the question of marijuana, the picture is less clear. While many parents may have been opposed to the legalization of marijuana when first confronted with the issue, their opinion may not be completely stable over time—perhaps because the results of medical research on the effects of marijuana are inconclusive. Simply put, the problem is that to assert that parents have transmitted a political orientation to their children seems to imply that the parents have some relatively long-term commitment to that orientation. If parents called themselves Democrats in one election and Republicans in the next, it would make little sense, irrespective of which party the child identified with, to say that he or she learned the party attachment from the parents.

Even where parents have consistent views to pass on to their children, another serious problem remains. Again, the issues raised by this problem are too complex to discuss fully here, but you should be aware of the problem in drawing conclusions from your data analysis. The problem concerns exactly what we mean when we say that parents and children agree in their political views. For party identification in 1965, for example, we found 57.3 percent of parent-child pairs in agreement. Does this mean that the party identification of 57.3 percent of the children in the sample was "caused" by parents? Probably not! If we tested the students in your class, for instance, we would find that all of them can read. If we tested all of their parents, we would probably find that their parents can read too. Would we conclude that their parents "caused" your classmates to be able to read? Unless some of them received all of their education at home, your answer would be: "No! My classmates learned to read at school."

The same logic can be applied to parent and child orientations towards politics. To say that parents and children prefer the same political party does not necessarily mean that the parents absolutely had to be the ones who taught the child his or her political preference. It could have been Aunt Matilda, or a ninth grade teacher, or any number of other people. In fact, in the most extreme situation, children may sometimes teach political opinions to parents. In any case, all that can be said when we find parent-child agreement on political questions is that we tentatively believe that parents transmitted their political opinions to their children. We believe this because it makes good intuitive sense that parents serve as teachers for their children. We are tentative about it because we recognize that there may be several other reasons for agreement that we simply have not had the opportunity to test.

What can we say about the 42.6 percent of the parent-child pairs who did not identify with the same political party? It seems safe to assert that these parents did not "cause" the party identification of their child. Again, thinking about the example of reading ability, if the child cannot read but the parent can, it makes a good deal of sense to say that the parent did not teach his child to read. But, even with this obvious inference, we must be cautious. It is possible that the child has "rebelled" against parental views, always adopting the opposite position from that of the parents. Previous research, though, has shown that rebellion is rare where political values are concerned.[21]

---

[21] Lane, *op. cit.*; and Russell Middleton and Snell Putney, "Political Expression of Adolescent Rebellion," *American Journal of Sociology*, 5 (March 1963), pp. 527-535.

Exercise No. 4: Parent-Child Agreement in 1965

1. Turn to the codebook at the back of the volume. Several political variables are listed there for parents and children in 1965. Choose one 1965 political variable on which you think most parents and children probably agreed with one another. Now choose a political variable from the 1965 data on which you think parents and children probably did not agree.
2. Why do you think that children and parents are likely to agree or to disagree on the variables you have selected?
3. Using your computer, generate a crosstab table that shows frequencies, total-percentages, and column-percentages. (NOTE: The column variable should be parent opinion and the row variable should be child opinion for both of the variables that you have selected.)
4. Answer questions a-d for *both variables,* the one where you expect high agreement and the one where you expect low agreement.
   a. What percentage of the parent-child pairs agree? What percentage of the parent-child pairs disagree?
   b. Are these the results that you expect? If the answer is "no", what are some reasons why you did not get the results you were expecting?
   c. What is the *pattern* of transmission in each of the columns?
   d. What, if anything, do these patterns of transmission tell you about the way in which young people were being socialized into the political system in 1965?

Some Alternative Measures of Agreement

When we use the total-percentages to determine what percentage of the parent-child pairs agree, the result is a simple summary measure of agreement which can be compared across a variety of political orientations. This percent agreement measure should have a great deal of intuitive appeal. It is easy to interpret and very simple to calculate.

Unhappily, the percent agreement measure has a major drawback. The percentage of parent-child pairs who agree depends on two things—(1) how much agreement there really is and (2) how many rows and columns are in the table. The first is fine. It is exactly what we want our measure of agreement to reflect. The second—the number of rows and columns—creates the problem. When the percentage agreement depends on the number of rows and columns, we cannot compare the agreement score for a table with two rows and two columns to that for a table with three rows and three columns. The percent agreement score, then, is affected by how fine our measurement categories are.

As an example of what we mean, let us suppose that party identification is measured in two different ways: the first by dividing respondents into Democrats, Independents, or Republicans; the second by dividing them into Independents or partisans. The resulting tables for parents and children in 1965 would look like this:

Table 5
Measuring Agreement for a Three-Category Party Identification Variable

| | | Parent | | |
		Democrat	Independent	Republican
Child	Democrat	x		
	Independent		x	
	Republican			x

Table 6
Measuring Agreement for a Two-Category Party Identification Variable

| | | Parent | |
		Independent	Partisan
Child	Independent	x	
	Partisan		x

The agreement cells are indicated by X's. It is much "easier" to obtain a high agreement score in Table 6 than in Table 5. Think about it like this. Do you recall the example of how to construct a cross-tabulation table earlier in the text, in which you dropped marbles into boxes? Suppose now that someone put a blindfold on you, gave you a bag of 100 marbles and told you to drop the marbles into the cells of the table in front of you. If the table were Table 6, how many marbles would you expect to find in each cell after you had dropped all of them? The odds are that about one-fourth (25) of the marbles would be in each cell. If you repeated the experiment with Table 5, you might well expect that about one-ninth (11) of the marbles would be in each cell. Now if you think of each marble as an "agreement" you can see that agreement will be much higher for Table 6 than for Table 5 even though you have dropped marbles randomly.

The same logic applies to measuring agreement in the Jennings data. If the table has two rows and two columns (a 2x2 table), it will have four cells. By chance alone, we would expect one-fourth of all the parent-child pairs to fall into each cell. If the table has three rows and three columns (a 3x3 table), it will have nine cells. In this case, we would expect only one-ninth of the parent-child pairs to be in each cell. If we calculated the agreement scores on these two "chance" tables, we would find that there is 50

33

percent agreement in the 2x2 table, but only 33 percent agreement in the 3x3 table.

This problem will not bother us too much in our analysis of the Jennings data because most variables have three categories and most tables are 3x3. Nevertheless, we can use our knowledge about the size of the table to modify the percent agreement measure so that it can be compared across tables of different sizes. In Table 5, with three rows and three columns, one-third of the cells are agreement cells. In Table 6, one-half of the cells are agreement cells. If we take the corresponding percentages—33.3 percent and 50.0 percent, respectively—as the agreement we would expect by chance alone, we can calculate a new measure which gives an indication of how much the agreement in a table differs from chance. We can call this measure the *adjusted percent agreement* score. For the percentages in Table 3 we would calculate it as follows:

$$\begin{array}{r} 57.3\% \text{ actual agreement} \\ -\ 33.3\% \text{ agreement by chance} \\ \hline 24.0\% \text{ adjusted percent agreement} \end{array}$$

Thus, for party identification in 1965, there is 24 percent more agreement that we would expect by randomly dropping "agreement marbles" into the cells.

While the adjusted percent agreement measure is an improvement over percent agreement, even it has a problem. It fails to take into account the *extent* of disagreement between parents and their children. Both the percent agreement score and its adjusted value would be the same if, say, half the younger generation agreed with its parent and the other half disagreed—regardless of how sharp the disagreement was. In the 3x3 table for party identification disagreeing offspring of Independent parents can move no more than one step away, either to Democrat or to Republican. But the sons and daughters of Democrats and Republicans can move one step to Independent or two steps to the opposite party. As we have seen, a two-step move is quite rare. One might feel that an agreement measure ought to score two-step disagreements more heavily than one-step disagreements. The scores presented so far do not.

There is an agreement score which avoids these troubles. The measure is called Kendall's tau-b. It can be used with tables of any size, if they have an equal number of rows and columns, and it will always be comparable from one table to another. Furthermore, the greater number of steps of departure from agreement, the more heavily such departures are weighted in the coefficient's calculation.

Tau-b always appears as a decimal fraction between + 1.00 for perfect agreement (*all* cases in the diagonal of agreement) and -1.00 for perfect *dis*agreement. In the party identification case, perfect disagreement would mean that all children of Democrats or of Republicans switched to the *opposite* party, while all children of Independents remained Independent. A tau-b of 0 (or close to 0) means that there is only a "chance relationship" between the party identification of the parent and that of the son or daughter—as if children choose their party by drawing a slip, while blindfolded, out of a hat. The only restriction on the drawing would be that we must put into the hat the proper "marginal percentage" of paper slips for each of the three possible identifications. We would still end up with the same number of Democrats, Independents, and Republicans; but the children of Democrats would be *just as likely* as the children of Republicans to end up Republican, and so on. In such a situation, it is obvious that parental party identification has no effect on the party identification of the children.

The 1965 data presented in Tables 2, 3, and 4 show, as we have seen, considerable agreement between parent and child on party identification. Tau-b for the tables is .48. (Since Tables 3 and 4 merely present the data from Table 2 in a different fashion, using total and column percentages, the tau-b will be the same for each.) A coefficient this high in value indicates "a strong relationship" between parents and children. Tables 7 and 8, later, show the data for 1973; the tau-b for these tables is .35, indicating a "moderately strong relationship" between parents and children. A tau-b of .20 or less would indicate a "weak relationship" or, if it were very close to zero, no relationship at all. Notice that a negative tau-b means disagreement: a tau-b of —.48 would suggest that children made a point of being different from their parents. Such disagreement is what is suggested by the word "rebellion."

A second correlation coefficient, Somers' D, is an even better measure for our purposes, because its value is not artificially reduced when the marginals are heavily unbalanced—i.e., where a very small number of re-spondents is in one of the categories. This makes it directly analogous to the percent agreement measure discussed above, with the added virtue that it can be compared across tables of different sizes. Like tau-b, Somers' D varies between +1.00 and —1.00, with a value of zero indicating no relationship. Somers' D, however, is not as familiar a measure as tau-b and, as a result, is not calculated by all computer programs.[22]

If your computer calculates tau-b and/or Somers' D you may wish to use one of them in lieu of percentage agreement in the exercises that follow.

---

[22] The mathematical bases for Kendall's tau-b and Somers' D are too complicated to be considered here. Explanations of them, particularly the more common tau-b measure, may be found in most statistics books. One good source is Hubert M. Blalock, Jr., *Social Statistics* (New York: McGraw-Hill, 1972), pp. 418-426.

IV. THE DURABILITY OF PARENT-CHILD AGREEMENT

Introduction

In the preceding section, we examined the extent to which parents and their children shared common political views in 1965—a time when many of the children who participated in the study were on the brink of leaving the home environment. After graduation, some stayed at home, some went on to college, others to the military, and still others into marriages or jobs. Many encountered new environments and ideas. Nor did all of the parents who participated in the 1965 phase of the study stand still—though their lives probably did not change as much as those of their children in the period after 1965.

The political world also underwent considerable change between 1965 and 1973. The Vietnam conflict raged throughout the last half of the decade. With it came student strikes, demonstrations, and sit-ins on hundreds of college campuses. With it also came the assignment of thousands of young Americans to military duty in Vietnam. The latter half of the 1960's was also a time of protest and violence on the civil rights front. In presidential politics, young people were mobilized to an unusual degree in the McCarthy, McGovern, and even Wallace movements. Then came Watergate, an event which was just emerging as important when respondents were interviewed in the Winter of 1973.

Changes in Parent-Child Agreement on Political Orientations

When you think about the 1965 high school seniors and their parents, what would you guess might have happened to their political views in the eight-year period between 1965 and 1973? There are several patterns of change (or the lack of it) that might have affected the level of agreement between parents and children. If you look back at the patterns of change that are discussed in Part II, you might get some ideas about what they are. Parents and their children might have grown farther apart during the eight-year period, so that there is less agreement. Or, they might have grown closer together, so that there is more agreement. Finally, they may have stayed at the same level of agreement. Additionally, we must keep in mind that the pattern of parent-child change over time may vary from one political orientation to another. For example, children may have come finally to agree

37

with their parents' feelings of cynicism but have decided that they prefer a different political party from that of their parents.

Underlying all of this, we are asking the question: "Is the political socialization that children have received by their senior year of high school something that remains unaltered throughout their lives?" If parents and children do change their opinions, how is that likely to affect the extent to which they agree or disagree about politics?

Before we begin to address directly this question of the durability of parent-child agreement, let us pause for a moment to consider the ways in which new environments might serve to influence a person's political ideas and opinions. Take the example of a person, perhaps like yourself, who has left home to attend college. Many college graduates you talk to will tell about the experience of having some of their views challenged by their new friends or professors. If those views were very strongly inculcated in the home environment, the experience of having them seriously challenged can be disturbing. How, then, does the maturing individual reconcile the demands for change from his new environment and the demand for stability from his old environment? The answer is, it depends.

Let's take a hypothetical example and see how it might depend. Suppose that Sally Freshman came from a Republican home. As we might have guessed, Sally is a Republican. The first thing Sally does is sign up for the Introductory Political Science course. To her dismay her professor turns out to be a liberal Democrat. Throughout the course, Sally's professor keeps giving her information which suggests that Republicans are the "bad guys" and the Democrats are the "good guys." In addition, she finds out that most of her classmates are Democrats. What will happen to Sally's partisan views? Well, it probably depends on the strength of her attachment to the Republican Party. If it is strong enough, Sally may go to the trouble to dig up counter arguments that tell her the Republicans are really the "good guys." Or she may simply argue that "all Political Science professors are stupid anyway." Another alternative is that Sally may simply live with all the inconsistencies saying that "Democrats may be 'good guys', but I'm a Republican just the same." Finally, she may actually begin to lean more and move towards the Democratic party. She will probably be more likely to change her old views if she likes her professor and if many of her classmates—with whom she interacts frequently—reinforce the idea that it is really the Democrats who are the "good guys."[23]

Obviously, this example might easily be extended to a variety of life experiences an individual could undergo. Service in the military, a new job, marriage, divorce, new friends, living in a new region of the country, or any of a number of other life experiences might confront children, or even their

---

[23] In reality, socialization researchers have found little evidence that professors influence students very much. See Albert Somit, Joseph Tanenhaus, Walter H. Wilke, and Rita W. Cooley, "The Effect of the Introductory Political Science Course on Student Attitudes toward Personal Political Participation," *American Political Science Review, 52 (December, 1958)*, pp. 1129-1132. Rather, the strongest effects of the college experience may be attributed to friends. See Theodore Newcomb, Richard Flacks, Kathryn Koenig, and Donald Warwick, *Persistence and Change* (New York: Wiley, 1967).

parents, with pressure to change beliefs learned earlier in life.

Now that some of the reasons why people might change their political views have been considered, let us examine the effect of the passage of time on the durability of parent-child agreement on party identification.

In Tables 7 and 8, parent party identification in 1973 is cross-tabulated with child party identification in 1973. Note that we have not given the frequency table. In its place, we have given you the total number of cases for the table showing total percentages (N = 1035) and the number of cases in each column for the column percentage table (N = 452, 274, and 309, respectively). With the N for Table 7 you could calculate the frequency table by multiplying each percentage in the table by the total number of cases and dividing by 100—for the cell in row one and column one, 22.1 x 1035 ÷ 100 = 229. The column percentages in Table 8 may be used in the same way. You could get the number of cases in row one and column one by 50.7 x 452 ÷ 100 = 229.

If you compare the table showing parent-child agreement in 1965 (Table 3) with Table 7, you will find that the level of agreement between parents and children declined over 10 percent in the period from 1965 to 1973. Tau-b, at the same time, went from .48 to .35. Thus, it appears that parents and children moved a little farther apart as they grew older. If you compare the 1965 and 1973 marginals, you can see what happened. Many of the children (i.e., 40.3 percent) identified with the Democratic party in 1965. Slightly over one-third (36.8 percent) identified as Independents. Just over one-fifth (22.9 percent) identified as Republicans. By 1973, this pattern had changed substantially—six percent fewer were Democrats (34.4 percent); 11 percent more were Independents (47.6 percent); and five percent fewer were Republiians (17.8 percent). Clearly, many of the children moved from a partisan to an independent position during the eight-year period. There was change in the parents too between 1965 and 1973. But it was not nearly as pronounced as that of the children. The percentage of Democratic parents dropped by less than three percent (46.2 percent to 43.7 percent). The percentage of Independent parents increased by only one percent (25.5 percent to 26.4 percent). Finally the percentage of Republican parents increased by less than two percent (28.2 percent to 29.8 percent).

Now if many children moved toward an Independent identification while a few parents moved toward Republican or Independent identifications, what would you expect to have happened to the levels of parent-child agreement? If your guess is that there would have been fewer Democratic pairs, more Independent pairs, and fewer Republican pairs, you are correct. Compare the Democrat-Democrat, Independent-Independent and Republican-Republican cells between 1965 and 1973 and see for yourself.

Notice that when we compare the marginals for parents to the marginals for children (that is, when in Table 7 we compare the percentage Democrat, Independent, and Republican in the parent group to the corresponding children's group percentages at the right margin of the table), we are seeing

Table 7
Total-Percentage for Parent-Child Party Identification in 1973

		Parent			
		Democrat	Independent	Republican	Total
	Democrat	22.1	7.7	4.6	34.4
Child	Independent	18.8	14.4	14.4	47.6
	Republican	2.7	4.3	10.8	17.8
	Total	43.6	26.4	29.8	100.0 (N=1035)

only part of the evidence of disagreement. The comparison of the marginals tells the *minimum* amount of disagreement there must be between *individual* parents and children. But if a Republican parent has a Democrat child, and that disagreement is "cancelled" by a Democrat parent with a Republican child, then these two cases of disagreement will not show up in a comparison of the marginals.

A comparison of the marginals tells us, then, what net changes have been registered in the distribution of partisanship for each group. How those marginal (or what are commonly called aggregate) changes came about can only be determined by looking at the interior cells of the table—at the agreement levels of parent-child pairs. You might convince yourself of this by seeing how many different cell entries you can place in Table 7 while retaining the original marginals.

Changes in the Differential Transmission of Political Orientations

Now, what about the patterns of transmission in 1973? What group of parents would you expect to have shown the highest level of agreement with their children in 1973—Democrats, Independents or Republicans? If you guessed Independents again, you are correct. Look at the columns of Table 8, and you will see that 54.4 percent of the children of 1973 Independent parents were also Independents, while slightly fewer children of Democratic parents were Democrats. Agreement was lowest between Republican parents and their children.

If you now look back at the column-percentage table for 1965 (Table 4), you will notice that agreement between Democratic parents and their children declined by about 13 percent between 1965 and 1973 (i.e., it was 63.9 percent in 1965 and 50.7 percent in 1973). Among Independent parents and their children agreement increased by almost three percent and among Republican parents and their children, agreement decreased by

Table 8
Column-Percentages for Parent-Child Party Identification in 1973

		Parent		
		Democrat	Independent	Republican
	Democrat	50.7	29.2	15.5
Child	Independent	43.1	54.4	48.2
	Republican	6.2	16.4	36.2
	Total	100.0	100.0	100.0
	(N)	(452)	(274)	(309)

over 15 percent. As you have probably come to expect by now, when parents and children did not agree in 1973, it was largely because children had become Independents while parents clung to their partisan affiliations. Very few children of either Democratic or Republican parents actually declared themselves to be members of the opposite party. When children of 1973 Independent parents did identify with a political party, however, it was much more likely to be the Democratic than the Republican party—as was the case in 1965.

What do these patterns tell us about the socialization of political party attachments in the United States? Perhaps the first thing they suggest is that regardless of all the possibilities for personal and political change discussed earlier, socialization works to produce significant amounts of agreement between parents and their children even after the children have matured into adults. Second, a decay in the socialization process seems to have produced a generational effect such that the young are more likely to reject partisan identifications than their parents probably were at the same age. The consequences that this might have for the future of the American political system are open to speculation. It may, for example, signal the breakdown of the two-party system as more and more young people reject both Democrats and Republicans in favor of political independence. Or perhaps the increased identification of young people as Independents is only a temporary thing. They may yet move back to the political party of their parents. Only time will tell.

In the exercise that follows, you will be able to conduct your own analysis of change in levels and patterns of agreement and disagreement among parents and children. You may pick the political variables that interest you. But before you get to that exercise, you should think about what you expect to find based on your own experience. What patterns of change would you expect to find in regard to political cynicism, for example? What about political ideology? Or political information? What do the expected patterns of similarities and differences suggest about the future of American politics as the older generation leaves the political system and the younger generation takes over?

Exercise No. 5: The Durability of Parent-Child Agreement

1. Select two political variables from the codebook. The first should be a variable for which you think that parent-child agreement will have decreased between 1965 and 1973. The second variable should be one for which you think that parent-child agreement will not have decreased between 1965 and 1973.
2. Why do you expect these patterns?
3. Use your computer to generate crosstab tables on these variables for parents and children in both 1965 and 1973.
4. Answer the following questions for both variables you have selected:
   a. What is the percent agreement in 1965? What is the percent agreement in 1973?
   b. Does a comparison of agreement in 1965 and 1973 tend to confirm or disconfirm your expectations? If these expectations were not confirmed, why do you think they were not confirmed?
   c. Looking at the column percentages, what are the patterns of transmission that occur in both 1965 and 1973? How do these patterns differ in the two years?

Conclusion

You have now examined the fate of parent-child agreement in political views after the child has become an adult. On some political views, the parental influence has eroded noticeably—to a point where what agreement existed between parents and children in 1965 has virtually vanished. On other political views, parent-child agreement has held up, and in some cases, even increased during the eight-year interval between 1965 and 1973. Before moving on to consider changes in the two generations separately and some of the reasons for these changes, let us pause to raise two questions. What do our findings tell us about the "staying power" of parental socialization where political views are concerned? Is this conclusion one that may apply to any time period or is it restricted to the 1965-1973 time interval? An answer to the first question merely requires summary of the changes in agreement for all political orientations measured in this study. The second question, however, can be answered satisfactorily only by gathering data on other generations in other time periods. Both are questions worth thinking about in setting the data we have analyzed into a broader context of political socialization research.

V. ADVANCED EXERCISES IN POLITICAL SOCIALIZATION

The preceding parts of this package focused on differences and similarities in the political views of two generations, the transmission of political views from parents to children when the children have not yet left the home environment, and the durability of parent-child similarities as the child matures into adulthood. There are, however, several additional questions which may be examined with the Jennings data. The purpose of Part V is to suggest some of these questions and to provide instruction in the techniques required to answer them.

Reasons for Parent-Child Agreement and Disagreement

In Part III of this volume, we examined the level and patterns of agreement and disagreement between parents and children in 1965. You will recall that about 57 percent of the parent-child pairs agreed on their party identification. In the subsequent exercises, you examined agreement and disagreement between parents and children on several other political orientations. The question that was not raised at the time is "Why do some parents and children agree on their political orientations while others do not?"

While one can never answer this question to complete satisfaction, we can begin to establish some tentative answers by looking for variations in agreement levels among groups of parents and children with different characteristics or life experiences. For example, would you expect the children to agree more with their parents if the parents are highly educated or if they are uneducated? Or would the level of parental education make no difference? Consider another example. We know that the South has traditionally been very Democratic. Would you expect parent-child agreement on party identification to be higher in southern families than in northern families? Would you expect parent-child agreement to be higher among southerners where parents were members of the dominant Democratic party? How about the sex of the parent? Does it affect agreement rates? Do children agree more frequently with mothers or with fathers? Do they agree with mothers more often on some political orientations and more often with fathers on others?

These examples suggest how we should begin to answer the question "Why do some parents and children agree while others do not?" By looking at agreements and disagreements between different groups of parents and their children, we are able to say things like: "On political orientations A, B, and C, children are more likely to agree with their mothers, while on political orientation D, they are more likely to agree with their fathers." Or we might find that children and parents are more likely to agree on politics if the parents are highly educated than if the parents are not very highly educated. We will have examined agreement under two conditions in each case—for mothers and fathers, for educated and relatively uneducated parents.

The analysis performed here is exactly the same as that involved previously in analyzing parent-child agreement except that overall agreement or patterns of transmission will be compared among several tables. Technically, this is called "controlling." Deck 2 in the codebook contains a variety of control variables for your use. They range from such characteristics as sex, race, and education to experiences that the individual might have had between 1965 and 1973. If, for example, you wanted to examine the effect of parent's sex on parent-child agreement, you would have two tables to examine rather than one—i.e., a table for parents and children when the parent interviewed was the mother and a table for the parents and children when the parent interviewed was the father. You would then calculate two percent agreement measures and compare them across the two "control" groups.

The technical procedures for controlling are relatively easy to master. You need only to generate a separate parent-child crosstab table for each category of a control variable. Interpreting "controlled" relationships can be difficult, though, unless you know exactly what to look for. Basically, the control variable "works" (i.e., has an effect) if the relationships differ among the separate categories of the control variable. The greater these differences, the more impact the control has. Where there is little difference in the parent-child relationships among the various control categories, the control does not "work"—i.e., the control variable does not appear to affect the socialization process. The reasons why a control works or does not work are varied and far beyond the scope of this volume. Nonetheless, a little experience in the use of controls should enable you to identify some of these reasons.[24]

Tables 9 and 10 contain an example of the use of controls with the party identification data reported earlier in Table 3. The control variable is parental political interest in 1965 (V54). We hypothesize that the level of parental interest affects the socialization process in the following way: the more interested in politics the parent is, the more likely the child and parent are to share the same party identification. Greater parent interest in politics

---

[24] See Morris Rosenberg, *The Logic of Survey Analysis* (New York: Basic Books, 1968), for an extended discussion of the effects of controls.

Table 9

Total-Percentages for Parent-Child Party Identification in 1965,
Controlling for Political Interest·

1. Parent interested in politics most of the time (N = 530)

		Parent			
		Democrat	Independent	Republican	
	Democrat	27.9	6.2	3.0	37.2
Child	Independent	11.9	14.5	11.3	37.7
	Republican	3.4	4.2	17.5	25.1
		43.2	24.9	31.9	100.0

%AGREEMENT=59.9   TAU B= .52   SOMERS'D=.52

2. Parent sometimes interested in politics (N = 315)

		Parent			
		Democrat	Independent	Republican	
	Democrat	33.0	8.3	2.5	43.8
Child	Independent	13.7	12.7	8.9	35.2
	Republican	3.8	5.7	11.4	21.0
		50.5	26.7	22.9	100.0

%AGREEMENT=57.1   TAU B=.46   SOMERS'D=.47

3. Parent seldom interested in politics (N = 190)

		Parent			
		Democrat	Independent	Republican	
	Democrat	28.4	10.5	4.7	43.7
Child	Independent	15.3	10.5	10.5	36.3
	Republican	3.7	4.7	11.6	20.0
		47.4	25.8	26.8	100.0

%AGREEMENT=50.5   TAU B=.37   SOMERS'D=.37

surely leads to more political discussion within the family and to clearer parental cues about which party is the "right" party. These, in turn, should influence the child to adopt the parental partisan views. The data in Table 9 support our hypothesis. No matter which measure of agreement is used (see the summary below each table),[25] parent-child agreement declines as parental interest declines. Because the differences are not large, however,

---

[25] Note the similarities in the values of tau-b and Somers' D. Where the marginals are fairly well balanced (as they are here), these values will be virtually the same.

Table 10

Column-Percentages for Parent-Child Party Identification in 1965, Controlling for Political Interest

1. Parent interested in politics most of the time (N=530)

		Democrat	Parent Independent	Republican	
	Democrat	64.6	25.0	9.5	37.2
Child	Independent	27.5	58.3	35.5	37.7
	Republican	7.9	16.7	55.0	25.1
		100.0	100.0	100.0	100.0
		(229)	(132)	(169)	

2. Parent sometimes interested in politics (N=315)

		Democrat	Parent Independent	Republican	
	Democrat	65.4	31.0	11.1	43.8
Child	Independent	27.0	47.6	38.9	35.2
	Republican	7.5	21.4	50.0	21.0
		99.9	100.0	100.0	100.0
		(159)	(84)	(72)	

3. Parent seldom interested in politics (N=190)

		Democrat	Parent Independent	Republican	
	Democrat	60.0	40.8	17.6	43.7
Child	Independent	32.2	40.8	39.2	36.3
	Republican	7.8	18.4	43.1	20.0
		100.0	100.0	99.9	100.0
		(90)	(49)	(51)	

we must conclude that levels of parental political interest do not influence strongly the political socialization of partisanship. Even where parental interest is lowest, there is substantial agreement between parent and child. Similarly, where parental interest is highest, much disagreement remains.

The patterns of transmission may also be analyzed within each category of the control variable. One reasonable hypothesis with which to begin this analysis might be that the higher the level of parental interest, the more likely parents of each partisan persuasion will be to pass on their partisanship to their children. Table 10, which is merely Table 9 re-percentaged to the columns, provides the data needed to test this hypothesis. In two of three cases, the hypothesis is confirmed. Only for Democratic parents does political interest not have the anticipated effect. Otherwise, sizable differences in socialization success occur consistently across the levels of parental political interest. Perhaps the most interesting data in this table are those in the Independent column: where the parent is interested in politics most of the time, the child is more likely to become an Independent than to become a partisan. The ability of Independent parents to transmit their views to their children in this situation exceeds the success of Republican parents at any level of interest and approaches the successes registered by Democratic parents. Political interest has a substantial impact here.

Exercise No. 6: Finding Reasons for Parent-Child Agreement

1. Pick a 1965 political orientation from the Jennings data that is of interest to you. Select a control variable which might affect the extent to which parents and children agree and the patterns of transmission on this orientation.
2. What is your hypothesis about the effects of this control variable? Why?
3. Run the crosstab table for parents and children for each of the groups designated by the control variable.
4. Assessing both levels of agreement and patterns of transmission, decide whether your hypothesis is supported by the data. If it is not, what are some reasons why it might have been wrong?

Just as you have done for parent-child pairs in 1965, the Jennings data allow you to examine agreement and disagreement in 1973. Although there is no formal exercise, you may want to choose some political orientation and subject it to "control" conditions that are relevant to the 1973 pairs. You might even want to compare agreement and disagreement in 1965 and 1973 under various "control" conditions, but you should give considerable thought to such a complicated exercise before beginning.

Changes in Political Views, 1965-1973

In the exercises of Part IV, you examined the durability of parent-child agreement over the eight-year period from 1965 to 1973. You found that on some political variables, agreement remained relatively high, while on others it seemed to decline substantially. Why do you think that agreement levels changed? The obvious answer, of course, is that either the parents or the children or both changed during the eight-year period.

The analysis performed in Exercise No. 5 did not allow you to examine changes in either generation. Yet you probably had some guesses or even hypotheses about the nature of this change. If we use the Jennings data in another way, it is possible to examine the patterns of stability and instability in parent and child political views between 1965 and 1973. The process for doing this is the same as that used when we examined parent-child agreement. All that we need to do is to generate a crosstab table. The difference is in what goes into the table. Instead of cross-tabulating parents with children, we cross-tabulate children in 1973 with children in 1965 or parents in 1973 with parents in 1965.

The interpretation of the resulting tables is also largely the same as that employed in the examination of parent-child agreement. The only difference is that you are now asking; "How much did children (or parents) agree or disagree with *themselves* after eight years?" You may still use the percent agreement measure except that when you examine how much an individual agreed with himself over the eight-year span, it is best referred to as a *measure of stability*. Thus, if you find that 50 percent of the children still had the same party identification in 1973, we will say that 50 percent of the children were "stable" during that time period. We could call the percentage disagreement (i.e., 100—measure of stability) the measure of change. The adjusted percent agreement measure, Kendall's tau-b, and Somers' D may be applied to this situation as well.

Exercise No. 7: Who Changes More, Parents or Children?
1. Pick a political variable which has interested you throughout the exercises. Decide who you think will have changed more on this variable—parents or children.
2. What are the reasons for your hypothesis?
3. Run the crosstab tables for both children (1965 by 1973) and parents (1965 by 1973).
4. Decide whether your hypothesis has been supported. Where it is not supported, discuss why not.

Reasons for Changes in Political Views

In the first of these advanced exercises, you attempted to determine why agreement is higher among some pairs of parents and children than others. In the second advanced exercise, you assessed individual change among parents and children. In this final exercise, we want to apply the *logic* of the first advanced exercise to the change that you found in completing the second exercise. In particular, we want to ask the question "Why do children or parents change over time?"

This question should not be new to you. We have alluded to it on several occasions throughout the volume and have suggested many possible answers. You may recall, for example, the case of Sally Freshman with the liberal Political Science professor. Her college experiences challenged the partisan views she had learned from her parents. A variety of life experiences might explain why children change as they move from adolescence to adulthood—viz., marriage, college, etc.

In the exercise that follows you will choose a political orientation and compare the stability and change among children who encountered

48

differing life experiences after high school graduation. (In doing this, you will be "controlling" for life experience). You might, for example, decide to examine stability and change in party identification among children who did and did not get married. Your hypothesis might be: those who married after school graduation are more likely to change than those who did not marry. One reason for this might be that marriage brings the individual into direct confrontation with another set of political views—those of the spouse. In many cases, these political views will be similar to the individual's own, but there are other cases in which the political views will be conflictual. When faced with such political conflict, one of the married couple is likely to change. To test this hypothesis, you would generate two tables—one for party identification in 1965 and 1973 for children who are married and one for party identification in 1965 and 1973 for children who are not married.[26] For your hypothesis to be supported by the data, you would need to find more change (and less stability) among the children who are married than among children who are not married. With this particular hypothesis, you might go even one step further to examine the impact of spouse directly by controlling for spouse's party identification.

Exercise No. 8: Finding Reasons for Change in Children
1. Pick a political orientation that is of interest to you. Choose a life experience control variable that you think will affect the extent to which children changed their minds about that orientation.
2. What is your hypothesis concerning the effects of the control? Why?
3. Run the crosstab tables for the political orientation within each category of the life experience control variable.
4. Decide whether your hypothesis is supported. Where it is not supported, discuss why not.

You saw in the last exercise that parents also change, albeit generally not as much as their children. Although there is no assigned exercise, we have included some variables which might be useful in explaining "why" parents change. If you are interested in pursuing the question on your own, you can do so in a manner analogous to that used for children in Exercise No. 8.

Conclusion

You have now seen the variety of ways in which more sophisticated analysis may be performed with the Jennings study. Controls may be added to relationships examined earlier and changes in either parents or children may be examined in their own right. Each of these additions vastly increases the amount of complexity involved in manipulating the data. Yet

---

[26] To simplify this analysis, we have created variables which measure change directly (V118 to V130). They may be run against the control variable so that the entire relationship is contained in a single table.

this increased complexity is the price researchers must pay for more satisfactory explanations of political phenomena. If you have come this far in the socialization package, you have come a long way towards understanding the process of political socialization.

VI. BIBLIOGRAPHY

Campbell, Angus, Philip E. Converse, Warren E. Miller, and Donald E. Stokes, *The American Voter* (New York: Wiley, 1960).
(Chapters 6 and 7 contain the now classic analysis of the importance and the development of party identification for the American electorate. The study is based on a national sample of American adults in the 1952 and 1956 elections.)

Davies, James C., "The Family's Role in Political Socialization," *The Annals of the American Academy of Political and Social Science,* 361 (September, 1965), pp. 10-19.
(General discussion of the importance of the family, particularly the parents, in early political socialization.)

Dawson, Richard E. and Kenneth Prewitt, *Political Socialization* (Boston: Little, Brown, 1969).
(Good general text on political socialization.)

Dodge, Richard W. and Eugene S. Uyeki, "Political Affiliations and Imagery across Two Related Generations," *Midwest Journal of Political Science,* 6 (May, 1962), pp. 266-276.
(Comparison of the political views of several hundred university freshmen and their parents reveals a great deal of similarity between parents and their children but also some important differences.)

Easton, David and Jack Dennis, *Children in the Political System* (New York: McGraw-Hill, 1969).
(Study of the development of attitudes towards government during the grade school years. Emphasis is placed on the socialization of supportive attitudes. The study is based on interviews with white public school children in large metropolitan areas of the United States.)

Greenberg, Edward S. (ed.), *Political Socialization* (New York: Atherton Press, 1970).
(Collection of articles on political socialization research. Particularly good on socialization within minority groups and the development of dissent.)

Greenstein, Fred I., *Children and Politics* (New Haven: Yale University Press, 1965).
(Study of the political views of grade school children in New Haven, Connecticut. Particularly useful in its analysis of the roots of partisanship and in its examination of social class and sex differences in socialization.)

Hess, Robert and Judith Torney, *The Development of Political Attitudes in Children* (Chicago: Aldine Press, 1967).
(Study of the development of political orientations during the grade school years. Much of this development is attributed to the influence of schools. The data set is the same as that used by Easton and Dennis.)

Hyman, Herbert, *Political Socialization* (New York: Free Press, 1959)
(The beginnings of the field of "political socialization" date from this path-breaking book. It contains an exhaustive bibliography of political socialization research before 1960.)

Jaros, Dean, Herbert Hirsch, and Frederic J. Fleron, Jr., "The Malevolent Leader: Political Socialization in an American Sub-Culture," *American Political Science Review*, 62 (June, 1968), 564-575.
(Study of school children, grade school through high school, in a county in Appalachia. The attitudes of these children, particularly their negative feelings towards government, contrast sharply with those found in the Easton and Dennis study.)

Jennings, M. Kent and Richard G. Niemi, "Continuity and Change in Political Orientations: A Longtitudinal Study of Two Generations," Paper Delivered at the 1973 Annual Meeting of the American Political Science Association. Also published in the *American Political Science Review*, 69 (September, 1975).
(The differences in the political views of the parent and child generations in the Jennings study are discussed for both 1965 and 1973).

Jennings, M. Kent and Richard G. Niemi, *The Political Character of Adolescence* (Princeton, New Jersey: Princeton University Press, 1974).
(Book length analysis of the 1965 portion of the Jennings study. It includes substantial analysis of the transmission of political views from parents to children.)

Jennings, M. Kent and Richard G. Niemi, "Patterns of Political Learning," *Harvard Education Review*, 38 (Summer, 1968), pp. 443-467.
(Discussion of the learning of political orientations throughout the life cycle.)

Jennings, M. Kent and Richard G. Niemi, "The Transmission of Political Values from Parent to Child," *American Political Science Review*, 62 (March, 1968), pp. 169-184.
(Analysis of the 1965 portion of the Jennings study with a direct focus on the transmission of political views from parents to children. Also examines this transmission under selected control conditions.)

Lane, Robert E., "Fathers and Sons: Foundations of Political Belief," *American Sociological Review*, 24 (August, 1959), pp. 502-511.
(In-depth study of the impact of fathers on the political views of 15 working and lower middle class men. Theme of adolescent rebellion, among others, is explored.)

Langton, Kenneth P., *Political Socialization* (New York: Oxford University Press, 1969).
(Emphasis is on the contributions of the various agents of socializa-

tion—the parents, the school, the peer group. Contains a chapter also assessing the differential impact of mothers and fathers.)

Langton, Kenneth P. and M. Kent Jennings, "Political Socialization in the High School Civics Curriculum in the United States," *American Political Science Review*, 62 (September, 1968), pp. 852-867.
(Comparison of the contributions of the civics curriculum to the political learning of blacks and whites using the 1965 portion of the Jennings study.)

Lyons, Schley R., "The Political Socialization of Ghetto Children," *Journal of Politics*, 32 (May, 1970), pp. 288-304.
(Study of the development of cynicism and efficacy among black school children in a northern city.)

McClosky, Herbert and Harold E. Dahlgren, "Primary Group Influence on Party Loyalty," *American Political Science Review*, 53 (September, 1959), pp. 757-776.
(Study of the impact of family and friends on the political orientations of a sample of adults in Minneapolis and St. Paul.)

Merelman, Richard M., "The Development of Political Ideology: A Framework for the Analysis of Political Socialization," *American Political Science Review*, 63 (September, 1969), pp. 750-767.
(Discussion of the growth of ideological thinking in children. The approach utilized draws heavily on psychologists' theories of cognitive development.)

Miller, Arthur H., "Political Issues and Trust in Government: 1964-1970," *American Political Science Review*, 68 (September, 1974), pp. 951-972. (Examination of changes in trust or cynicism of American adults over the last decade.)

Newcomb, Theodore, Richard Flacks, Kathryn Koenig, and Donald Warwick, *Persistence and Change: Bennington College and Its Students after Twenty-Five Years* (New York: Wiley, 1967).
(Study of the impact of a small, liberal arts college on the political views of its students while they were in college and of the fate of these views some twenty-five years later.)

Niemi, Richard G., and Associates, *The Politics of Future Citizens: New Dimensions in the Political Socialization of Children* (San Francisco: Jossey-Bass Publishers, 1974).
(A set of original essays on a variety of topics—minority group socialization, changes in children's political views, and the kinds of changes which may occur in the early adult years.)

Sigel, Roberta S. (ed.), *Learning About Politics* (New York: Random House, 1970).
(Probably the most comprehensive collection of published articles on political socialization research.)

CODEBOOK

NOTE: Some of the questions listed in the following codebook have been changed slightly from their original form. All marginal frequencies are based on the unweighted data. In using this codebook, OSIRIS users and SPSS users working with a SAVE FILE should ignore deck and column references. In these cases, variables may be referenced by the variable identification number.

DECK	COLUMN	VARIABLE	VARIABLE DESCRIPTION INFORMATION
1	1	V1	C65 PARTY ID "Generally speaking, do you usually think of yourself as a Republican, a Democrat, an Independent, or what?" 425 1. Democrat 387 2. Independent 239 3. Republican 11 9. Missing Data
1	2	V2	P65 PARTY ID "Generally speaking, do you usually think of yourself as a Republican, a Democrat, an Independent, or what?" 481 1. Democrat 271 2. Independent 294 3. Republican 16 9. Missing Data
1	3	V3	C73 PARTY ID "Generally speaking, do you usually think of yourself as a Republican, a Democrat, an Independent, or what?" 361 1. Democrat 504 2. Independent 189 3. Republican 8 9. Missing Data
1	4	V4	P73 PARTY ID "Generally speaking, do you usually think of yourself as a Republican, a Democrat, an Independent, or what?" 456 1. Democrat 276 2. Independent 309 3. Republican 21 9. Missing Data
1	5	V5	C65 PRES PREF 64 "Whom did you prefer for President in the

DECK	COLUMN	VARIABLE	VARIABLE DESCRIPTION INFORMATION

1964 election?"
747 1. Democrat (Johnson)
283 2. Republican (Goldwater)
 32 9. Missing Data

| 1 | 6 | V6 | P65 PRES PREF 64 |

"Whom did you prefer for President in the 1964 election?"
675 1. Democrat (Johnson)
334 2. Republican (Goldwater)
 53 9. Missing Data

| 1 | 7 | V7 | C73 PRES PREF 72 |

"Whom did you prefer for President in the 1972 election?"
381 1. Democrat (McGovern)
566 2. Republican (Nixon)
115 9. Missing Data

| 1 | 8 | V8 | P73 PRES PREF 72 |

"Whom did you prefer for President in the 1972 election?"
297 1. Democrat (McGovern)
660 2. Republican (Nixon)
105 9. Missing Data

| 1 | 9 | V9 | C65 CONSERV PARTY |

"Generally speaking, is either one of the political parties more conservative than the other?"
163 1. Democrats more conservative
388 2. Neither, same
492 3. Republicans more conservative
 19 9. Missing Data

| 1 | 10 | V10 | P65 CONSERV PARTY |

"Generally speaking, is either one of the political parties more conservative than the other?"
119 1. Democrats more conservative
330 2. Neither, same
600 3. Republicans more conservative
 13 9. Missing Data

| 1 | 11 | V11 | C73 CONSERV PARTY |

"Generally speaking, is either one of the political parties more conservative than the other?"
121 1. Democrats more conservative
189 2. Neither, same

DECK	COLUMN	VARIABLE	VARIABLE DESCRIPTION INFORMATION

                        686 3. Republicans more conservative
                         66 9. Missing Data

1   12   V12   P73 CONSERV PARTY

"Generally speaking, is either one of the political parties more conservative than the other?"

111 1. Democrats more conservative
281 2. Neither, same
648 3. Republicans more conservative
 22 9. Missing Data

1   13   V13   C65 BEST GOV

"We find that people differ in how much faith and confidence they have in various levels of government. In your case, do you have more faith and confidence in the national government, the government of this state, or the local government around here?"

851 1. National
 19 2. Combination, none, or all equal
183 3. State, local
  9 9. Missing Data

1   14   V14   P65 BEST GOV

"We find that people differ in how much faith and confidence they have in various levels of government. In your case, do you have more faith and confidence in the national government, the government of this state, or the local government around here?"

531 1. National
 97 2. Combination, none, or all equal
384 3. State, local
 50 9. Missing Data

1   15   V15   C73 BEST GOV

"We find that people differ in how much faith and confidence they have in various levels of government. In your case, do you have more faith and confidence in the national government, the government of this state, or the local government around here?"

440 1. National
178 2. Combination, none, or all equal

DECK	COLUMN	VARIABLE	VARIABLE DESCRIPTION INFORMATION

430 3. State, local
14 9. Missing Data

1   16   V16   P73 BEST GOV
"We find that people differ in how much faith and confidence they have in various levels of government. In your case, do you have more faith and confidence in the national government, the government of this state, or the local government around here?"
362 1. National
288 2. Combination, none, or all equal
357 3. State, local
55 9. Missing Data

1   17   V17   C65 INTEGRATION
"Some people say that the government in Washington should see to it that white and black children are allowed to go to the same schools. Do you agree?"
679 1. Yes
97 2. Depends
212 3. No
74 9. Missing Data

1   18   V18   P65 INTEGRATION
"Some people say that the government in Washington should see to it that white and black children are allowed to go to the same schools. Do you agree?"
553 1. Yes
125 2. Depends
292 3. No
92 9. Missing Data

1   19   V19   C73 INTEGRATION
"Some people say that the government in Washington should see to it that white and black children are allowed to go to the same schools. Do you agree?"
487 1. Yes
151 2. Depends
351 3. No
73 9. Missing Data

1   20   V20   P73 INTEGRATION
"Some people say that the government in Washington should see to it that white and

DECK	COLUMN	VARIABLE	VARIABLE DESCRIPTION INFORMATION

black children are allowed to go to the same schools. Do you agree?"
398 1. Yes
138 2. Depends
401 3. No
125 9. Missing Data

| 1 | 21 | V21 | C65 PRAYER |

"Some people think that it is all right for the public schools to start each day with a prayer. Do you agree?"
611 1. Yes
271 2. No
180 9. Missing Data

| 1 | 22 | V22 | P65 PRAYER |

"Some people think that it is all right for the public schools to start each day with a prayer. Do you agree?"
770 1. Yes
166 2. No
126 9. Missing Data

| 1 | 23 | V23 | C73 PRAYER |

"Some people think that it is all right for the public schools to start each day with a prayer. Do you agree?"
594 1. Yes
301 2. No
167 9. Missing Data

| 1 | 24 | V24 | P73 PRAYER |

"Some people think that it is all right for the public schools to start each day with a prayer. Do you agree?"
784 1. Yes
156 2. No
122 9. Missing Data

| 1 | 25 | V25 | C65 TOLERANCE |

Combination of responses to the following questions:

"If a person wanted to make a speech in this community against churches and religion, should he be allowed to speak?" and "If a Communist were legally elected to some public office around here, should the people allow him to take office?"
100 1. Low (2 "no" responses)

DECK	COLUMN	VARIABLE	VARIABLE DESCRIPTION INFORMATION

579 2. Mid (response combinations not contained in 1 and 3)

378 3. High (2 "yes" responses)

5 9. Missing Data

1   26   V26   P65 TOLERANCE

Combination of responses to the following questions: "If a person wanted to make a speech in this community against churches and religion, should he be allowed to speak?" *and* "If a Communist were legally elected to some public office around here, should the people allow him to take office?"

226 1. Low (2 "no" responses)

526 2. Mid (response combinations not contained in 1 and 3)

281 3. High (2 "yes" responses)

29 9. Missing Data

1   27   V27   C73 TOLERANCE

Combination of responses to the following questions: "If a person wanted to make a speech in this community against churches and religion, should he be allowed to speak?" *and* "If a Communist were legally elected to some public office around here, should the people allow him to take office?"

46 1. Low (2 "no" responses)

382 2. Mid (response combinations not contained in 1 and 3)

620 3. High (2 "yes" responses)

14 9. Missing Data

1   28   V28   P73 TOLERANCE

Combination of responses to the following questions: "If a person wanted to make a speech in this community against churches and religion, should he be allowed to speak?" *and* "If a Communist were legally elected to some public office around here, should the people allow him to take office?"

196 1. Low (2 "no" responses)

433 2. Mid (response combinations not contained in 1 or 3)

DECK	COLUMN	VARIABLE	VARIABLE DESCRIPTION INFORMATION

406 3. High (2 "yes" responses)
 27 9. Missing Data

1   29   V29   C65 GOV WASTE $
"Do you think that people in the government waste the money we pay in taxes?"
203 1. Not much
602 2. Some
250 3. A lot
  7 9. Missing Data

1   30   V30   P65 GOV WASTE $
"Do you think that people in the government waste the money we pay in taxes?"
 78 1. Not much
485 2. Some
480 3. A lot
 19 9. Missing Data

1   31   V31   C73 GOV WASTE $
"Do you think that people in the government waste the money we pay in taxes?"
 22 1. Not much
390 2. Some
643 3. A lot
  7 9. Missing Data

1   32   V32   P73 GOV WASTE $
"Do you think that people in the government waste the money we pay in taxes?"
 39 1. Not much
307 2. Some
698 3. A lot
 18 9. Missing Data

1   33   V33   C65 TRUST GOV
"How much of the time do you think you can trust the government in Washington to do what is right?"
446 1. About always
530 2. Most of the time
 82 3. Only sometimes
  4 9. Missing Data

1   34   V34   P65 TRUST GOV
"How much of the time do you think you can trust the government in Washington to do what is right?"
196 1. About always
629 2. Most of the time

DECK	COLUMN	VARIABLE	VARIABLE DESCRIPTION INFORMATION

216   3. Only sometimes
21   9. Missing Data

| 1 | 35 | V35 | |

C73 TRUST GOV
"How much of the time do you think you can trust the government in Washington to do what is right?"
115   1. About always
587   2. Most of the time
352   3. Only sometimes
8   9. Missing Data

| 1 | 36 | V36 | |

P73 TRUST GOV
"How much of the time do you think you can trust the government in Washington to do what is right?"
106   1. About always
516   2. Most of the time
408   3. Only sometimes
32   9. Missing Data

| 1 | 37 | V37 | |

C65 GOV CROOKED
"How many of the people running the government are crooked?"
315   1. Hardly any
553   2. Not many
186   3. Quite a few
8   9. Missing Data

| 1 | 38 | V38 | |

P65 GOV CROOKED
"How many of the people running the government are crooked?"
268   1. Hardly any
500   2. Not many
251   3. Quite a few
43   9. Missing Data

| 1 | 39 | V39 | |

C73 GOV CROOKED
"How many of the people running the government are crooked?"
158   1. Hardly any
524   2. Not many
357   3. Quite a few
23   9. Missing Data

| 1 | 40 | V40 | |

P73 GOV CROOKED
"How many of the people running the government are crooked?"
259   1. Hardly any
435   2. Not many

DECK	COLUMN	VARIABLE	VARIABLE DESCRIPTION INFORMATION

313 3. Quite a few

  55 9. Missing Data

1   41   V41   C65 GOV SMART

"Do you feel that almost all of the people running the government are smart people who usually know what they are doing, or do you think that quite a few of them don't seem to know what they are doing?"

907 1. Know what they are doing

143 2. Don't know what they are doing

  12 9. Missing Data

1   42   V42   P65 GOV SMART

"Do you feel that almost all of the people running the government are smart people who usually know what they are doing, or do you think that quite a few of them don't seem to know what they are doing?"

749 1. Know what they are doing

273 2. Don't know what they are doing

  40 9. Missing Data

1   43   V43   C73 GOV SMART

"Do you feel that almost all of the people running the government are smart people who usually know what they are doing, or do you think that quite a few of them don't seem to know what they are doing?"

734 1. Know what they are doing

279 2. Don't know what they are doing

  49 9. Missing Data

1   44   V44   P73 GOV SMART

"Do you feel that almost all of the people running the government are smart people who usually know what they are doing, or do you think that quite a few of them don't seem to know what they are doing?"

637 1. Know what they are doing

386 2. Don't know what they are doing

  39 9. Missing Data

1   45   V45   C65 ALL OR FEW

"Would you say the government is pretty much run by a few big interests looking out for themselves or that it is run for the benefit of all the people?"

896 1. Benefits all

DECK	COLUMN	VARIABLE	VARIABLE DESCRIPTION INFORMATION

| | | | 126 2. For the few |
| | | | 40 9. Missing Data |

1   46   V46   P65 ALL OR FEW
"Would you say the government is pretty much run by a few big interests looking out for themselves or that it is run for the benefit of all the people?"

741 1. Benefits all
233 2. For the few
 88 9. Missing Data

1   47   V47   C73 ALL OR FEW
"Would you say the government is pretty much run by a few big interests looking out for themselves or that it is run for the benefit of all the people?"

395 1. Benefits all
599 2. For the few
 68 9. Missing Data

1   48   V48   P73 ALL OR FEW
"Would you say the government is pretty much run by a few big interests looking out for themselves or that it is run for the benefit of all the people?"

429 1. Benefits all
519 2. For the few
114 9. Missing Data

1   49   V49   C65 CYNICISM
Combination of responses to the preceding five questions—variables V29, V33, V37, V41, and V45. Middle categories, where used, are counted as neither "cynical" nor "trusting" responses.

681 1. Low (at least 3 "trusting" and no more than 1 "cynical" responses)
272 2. Mid (response combinations not contained in 1 or 3)
 81 3. High (at least 3 "cynical" and no more than 1 "trusting" responses)
 28 9. Missing Data

1   50   V50   P65 CYNICISM
Combination of responses to the preceding five questions—variables V30, V34, V38, V42, and V46. Middle categories, where used, are counted as neither "cynical"

nor "trusting" responses.
460 1. Low (at least 3 "trusting" and no more than 1 "cynical" responses)
298 2. Mid (response combinations not contained in 1 or 3)
218 3. High (at least 3 "cynical" and no more than 1 "trusting" responses)
86 9. Missing Data

1	51	V51	C73 CYNICISM

Combination of responses to the preceding five questions—variables V31, V35, V39, V43, and V47. Middle categories, where used, are counted as neither "cynical" nor "trusting" responses.
212 1. Low (at least 3 "trusting" and no more than 1 "cynical" responses)
368 2. Mid (response combinations not contained in 1 or 3)
404 3. High (at least 3 "cynical" and no more than 1 "trusting" responses)
78 9. Missing Data

1	52	V52	P73 CYNICISM

Combination of responses to the preceding five questions—variables V32, V36, V40, V44, and V48. Middle categories, where used, are counted as neither "cynical" nor "trusting" responses.
186 1. Low (at least 3 "trusting" and no more than 1 "cynical" responses)
349 2. Mid (response combinations not contained in 1 or 3)
373 3. High (at least 3 "cynical" and no more than 1 "trusting" responses)
154 9. Missing Data

1	53	V53	C65 INTEREST

"How often would you say that you follow what is going on in government and public affairs?"
441 1. Most of the time
469 2. Sometimes
152 3. Seldom
0 9. Missing Data

1	54	V54	P65 INTEREST

"How often would you say that you follow

what is going on in government and public affairs?"

536 1. Most of the time
324 2. Sometimes
201 3. Seldom
  1 9. Missing Data

| 1 | 55 | V55 | C73 INTEREST |

"How often would you say that you follow what is going on in government and public affairs?"

519 1. Most of the time
391 2. Sometimes
151 3. Seldom
  1 9. Missing Data

| 1 | 56 | V56 | P73 INTEREST |

"How often would you say that you follow what is going on in government and public affairs?"

588 1. Most of the time
310 2. Sometimes
164 3. Seldom
  0 9. Missing Data

| 1 | 57 | V57 | C65 LOCALISM |

Four levels of public affairs—international, national, state, and local—ranked in order of respondent's interest in them.

548 1. Low (ranked international and national above all others)
173 2. Mid (rankings not contained in 1 or 3)
 87 3. High (ranked state and local above all others)
254 9. Missing Data

| 1 | 58 | V58 | P65 LOCALISM |

Four levels of public affairs—international, national, state, and local—ranked in order of respondent's interest in them.

271 1. Low (ranked international and national above all others)
223 2. Mid (rankings not contained in 1 or 3)
205 3. High (ranked state and local above all others)
363 9. Missing Data

66

DECK	COLUMN	VARIABLE	VARIABLE DESCRIPTION INFORMATION

1   59   V59   **C73 LOCALISM**
Four levels of public affairs—international, national, state, and local—ranked in order of respondent's interest in them.
447   1. Low (ranked international and national above all others)
227   2. Mid (rankings not contained in 1 or 3)
129   3. High (ranked state and local above all others)
259   9. Missing Data

1   60   V60   **P73 LOCALISM**
Four levels of public affairs—international, national, state, and local—ranked in order of respondent's interest in them.
217   1. Low (ranked international and national above all others)
266   2. Mid (rankings not contained in 1 or 3)
224   3. High (ranked state and local above all others)
355   9. Missing Data

1   61   V61   **C65 KNOWLEDGE**
Number of correct answers to a six question test on political affairs.
252   1. Low (no more than 2 correct answers)
477   2. Mid (3 or 4 correct answers)
321   3. High (more than 4 correct answers)
12   9. Missing Data

1   62   V62   **P65 KNOWLEDGE**
Number of correct answers to a six question test on political affairs.
165   1. Low (no more than 2 correct answers)
563   2. Mid (3 or 4 correct answers)
315   3. High (more than 4 correct answers)
19   9. Missing Data

1   63   V63   **C73 KNOWLEDGE**
Number of correct answers to a six question test on political affairs.

DECK	COLUMN	VARIABLE	VARIABLE DESCRIPTION INFORMATION

189 1. Low (no more than 2 correct answers)
399 2. Mid (3 or 4 correct answers)
275 3. High (more than 4 correct answers)
199 9. Missing Data

| 1 | 64 | V64 | P73 KNOWLEDGE |

Number of correct answers to a six question test on political affairs.
183 1. Low (no more than 2 correct answers)
476 2. Mid (3 or 4 correct answers)
319 3. High (more than 4 correct answers)
 84 9. Missing Data

| 1 | 65 | V65 | C65 EFFICACY |

Combination of responses to the following 2 questions: "Is voting the only way that people can have any say about how the government runs things?" *and* "Is politics and government sometimes so complicated that a person can't really understand what's going on?"
208 1. Low ("yes" to both questions)
513 2. Mid (response combinations not contained in 1 or 3)
335 3. High ("no" to both questions)
 6 9. Missing Data

| 1 | 66 | V66 | P65 EFFICACY |

Combination of responses to the following 2 questions: "Is voting the only way that people can have any say about how the government runs things?" *and* "Is politics and government sometimes so complicated that a person can't really understand what's going on?"
401 1. Low ("yes" to both questions)
432 2. Mid (response combinations not contained in 1 or 3)
221 3. High ("no" to both questions)
 8 9. Missing Data

| 1 | 67 | V67 | C73 EFFICACY |

Combination of responses to the following

68

DECK	COLUMN	VARIABLE	VARIABLE DESCRIPTION INFORMATION

2 questions: "Is voting the only way that people can have any say about how the government runs things?" *and* "Is politics and government sometimes so complicated that a person can't really understand what's going on?"

267 1. Low ("yes" to both questions)
534 2. Mid (response combinations not contained in 1 or 3)
251 3. High ("no" to both questions)
 10 9. Missing Data

1	68	V68	P73 EFFICACY

Combination of responses to the following 2 questions: "Is voting the only way that people can have any say about how the government runs things?" *and* "Is politics and government sometimes so complicated that a person can't really understand what's going on?"

477 1. Low ("yes" to both questions)
410 2. Mid (response combinations not contained in 1 or 3)
160 3. High ("no" to both questions)
 15 9. Missing Data

1	69	V69	C65 RELIGION

Religious preference of respondent.
735 1. Protestant
249 2. Catholic
 61 3. Other, none
 17 9. Missing Data

1	70	V70	P65 RELIGION

Religious preference of respondent.
755 1. Protestant
241 2. Catholic
 63 3. Other, none
  3 9. Missing Data

1	71	V71	C73 RELIGION

Religious preference of respondent.
651 1. Protestant
219 2. Catholic
190 3. Other, none
  2 9. Missing Data

1	72	V72	P73 RELIGION

Religious preference of respondent

DECK	COLUMN	VARIABLE	VARIABLE DESCRIPTION INFORMATION
			739 1. Protestant
			235 2. Catholic
			84 3. Other, none
			4 9. Missing Data
1	73		BLANK
1	74		BLANK
1	75-78	V73	PAIR ID (unique number for each parent-child pair)
1	79	V74	STUDY NUMBER (2)
1	80	V75	DECK NUMBER (1)
2	1	V76	C65 SEX
			Sex of the respondent.
			526 1. Male
			536 2. Female
2	2	V77	P65 SEX
			Sex of the respondent.
			448 1. Male
			614 2. Female
2	3	V78	C65 RACE
			Race of the respondent.
			966 1. White
			83 2. Black
			13 9. Missing Data
2	4	V79	P65 RACE
			Race of the respondent.
			965 1. White
			83 2. Black
			14 9. Missing Data
2	5	V80	P65 EDUCATION OF HOH
			Years of formal education for head of household.
			238 1. None to 8
			516 2. High school
			155 3. Some college
			147 4. BA or more
			6 9. Missing Data
2	6	V81	P65 FAM INCOME
			Estimated family income in thousands of dollars.
			646 1. Low (1-10)
			239 2. Mid (10-15)
			149 3. High (15+)
			28 9. Missing Data

DECK	COLUMN	VARIABLE	VARIABLE DESCRIPTION INFORMATION

| 2 | 7 | V82 | P65 C-P CLOSENESS |

"How close would you say that you are to your child?"

590 1. Very close
435 2. Pretty close
  35 3. Not very close
   2 9. Missing Data

| 2 | 8 | V83 | P65 SPOUSE PARTY ID |

"Generally speaking, does your spouse think of (himself/herself) as a Republican, a Democrat, an Independent, or what?"

457 1. Democrat
174 2. Independent
285 3. Republican
146 9. Missing Data

| 2 | 9 | V84 | C65 REGION |

Region of parent and child.

272 1. South and Border
790 2. Non-South
   0 9. Missing Data

| 2 | 10 | V85 | C73 REGION |

Region of the respondent.

302 1. South and Border
760 2. Non-South
   0 9. Missing Data

| 2 | 11 | V86 | P73 REGION |

Region of the respondent.

313 1. South and Border
749 2. Non-South
   0 9. Missing Data

| 2 | 12 | V87 | C73 EDUCATION |

Years of formal education for the respondent.

   0 1. None to 8
369 2. High school
291 3. Some college
399 4. BA or more
   3 9. Missing Data

| 2 | 13 | V88 | P73 EDUCATION OF HOH |

Years of formal education for head of household.

237 1. None to 8
497 2. High school

71

DECK	COLUMN	VARIABLE	VARIABLE DESCRIPTION INFORMATION

			171 3. Some college
			151 4. BA or more
			6 9. Missing Data
2	14	V89	C73 FAM INCOME Estimated family income in thousands of dollars. 352 1. Low (1-10) 290 2. Mid (10-15) 221 3. High (15+) 199 9. Missing Data
2	15	V90	P73 FAM INCOME Estimated family income in thousands of dollars. 314 1. Low (1-10) 246 2. Mid (10-15) 396 3. High (15+) 106 9. Missing Data
2	16	V91	C73 SOCIAL CLASS "There's quite a bit of talk these days about different social classes. Most people say they belong either to the middle class or to the working class. What about you?" 355 1. Working 517 2. Middle 190 9. Missing Data
2	17	V92	P73 SOCIAL CLASS "There's quite a bit of talk these days about different social classes. Most people say they belong either to the middle class or to the working class. What about you?" 471 1. Working 500 2. Middle 91 9. Missing Data
2	18	V93	P73 C-P CONTACT "Could you tell me about how often you see your child?" 262 1. Every 2 to 3 months or less 349 2. Each month to each week 251 3. Twice a week or more 200 9. Missing Data
2	19	V94	C73 LIVES WITH P "Do you now live with your parent?" 759 1. Not with parent 126 2. With one or both

DECK	COLUMN	VARIABLE	VARIABLE DESCRIPTION INFORMATION

			177 9. Missing Data

2   20   V95   C73 DEMONSTRATIONS
"Have you ever taken part in a demonstration, protest march, or sit-in?"
175 1. Yes
884 2. No
3 9. Missing Data

2   21   V96   P73 DEMONSTRATIONS
"Have you ever taken part in a demonstration, protest march, or sit-in?"
26 1. Yes
1031 2. No
5 9. Missing Data

2   22   V97   C73 VIETNAM CHANGE
"Did our participation in the Vietnam war cause you to change any of your views about the United States?"
549 1. Yes
510 2. No
3 9. Missing Data

2   23   V98   P73 VIETNAM CHANGE
"Did our participation in the Vietnam war cause you to change any of your views about the United States?"
271 1. Yes
780 2. No
11 9. Missing Data

2   24   V99   C73 MARITAL STATUS
"What is your marital status?"
563 1. Married, cohabiting
499 2. Single, divorced, separated, or widowed
0 9. Missing Data

2   25   V100   C73 SPOUSE PARTY ID
"Generally speaking, does your spouse think of (himself/herself) as a Republican, a Democrat, an Independent, or what?"
216 1. Democrat
200 2. Independent
129 3. Republican
517 9. Missing Data

2   26   V101   C73 TALK W SPOUSE
"Do you and your spouse ever talk about any kind of public affairs and politics, that

is, anything to do with local, state, national, or international affairs?"
82 1. Very often
262 2. Pretty often
190 3. Seldom
63 4. Never
465 9. Missing Data

2 27 V102 C73 DISAGREE W SPOUSE
"Do you and your spouse ever disagree about anything having to do with public affairs and politics?"
44 1. Very often
220 2. Pretty often
101 3. Seldom
169 4. Never
528 9. Missing Data

2 28 V103 C73 COLLEGE MAJOR
"What was your college major?"
28 1. Natural sciences
100 2. Social sciences
74 3. Humanities and the arts
319 4. Other
541 9. Missing Data

2 29 V104 C73 COLLEGE GRADES
"What was your grade average in college?"
45 1. A
269 2. B
205 3. C
543 9. Missing Data

2 30 V105 C73 COLLEGE SATIS
"In general, how satisfied were you with your experience in college?"
214 1. Very satisfied
216 2. Somewhat satisfied
88 3. Somewhat dissatisfied
26 4. Very dissatisfied
518 9. Missing Data

2 31 V106 C73 COLLEGE CHALLENGE
"When you were in college, did you have any of your important beliefs or values challenged by fellow students, professors, something you read, or something that happened?"
248 1. Yes

302 2. No

512 9. Missing Data

2	32	V107	**C73 PERSONAL TRUST**

Combination of responses to the following questions: "Would you say that most people can be trusted?"; "Would you say that most of the time people try to be helpful?"; "Do you think that most people would try to take advantage of you if they got a chance?"

220 1. Low ("non-trusting" response to at least 2 questions, "depends" response to no more than 1 question)

397 2. Mid (response combinations not contained in 1 or 3)

428 3. High ("trusting" response to at least 2 questions, "depends" response to no more than 1 question)

17 9. Missing Data

2	33	V108	**C73 STRONGMINDEDNESS**

Combination of responses to the following questions: "When you get into an argument do you usually get your own way?"; "Do you have strong opinions about many things?"; "When you make up your mind about something is it pretty hard to argue you out of it?"

100 1. Low ("no" response to at least 2 questions, "depends" response to no more than 1 question)

522 2. Mid (response combinations not contained in 1 or 3)

254 3. High ("yes" response to at least 2 questions, "depends" response to no more than 1 question)

186 9. Missing Data

2	34	V109	**C73 ELECT ACTIVITY**

"Have you engaged in any of the following election activities: wearing a campaign button or putting a campaign sticker on your car, talking to family or friends, attending political meetings, giving money or buy-

ing tickets to help a party or candidate?"
402 1. None
475 2. Some (1 or 2 activities)
185 3. Lots (3 or 4 activities)
　0 9. Missing Data

2	35	V110	C65 FREE SPEECH

"If a person wanted to make a speech in this community against churches and religion, should he be allowed to speak?"
933 1. Yes
123 2. No
　6 9. Missing Data

2	36	V111	P65 FREE SPEECH

"If a person wanted to make a speech in this community against churches and religion, should he be allowed to speak?"
784 1. Yes
264 2. No
　14 9. Missing Data

2	37	V112	C73 FREE SPEECH

"If a person wanted to make a speech in this community against churches and religion, should he be allowed to speak?"
1001 1. Yes
　58 2. No
　　3 9. Missing Data

2	38	V113	P73 FREE SPEECH

"If a person wanted to make a speech in this community against churches and religion, should he be allowed to speak?"
810 1. Yes
242 2. No
　10 9. Missing Data

2	39	V114	C65 FREE ELECTIONS

"If a Communist were legally elected to some public office around here, should the people allow him to take office?"
404 1. Yes
647 2. No
　11 9. Missing Data

2	40	V115	P65 FREE ELECTIONS

"If a Communist were legally elected to some public office around here, should the people allow him to take office?"

DECK	COLUMN	VARIABLE	VARIABLE DESCRIPTION INFORMATION

316 1. Yes
724 2. No
22 9. Missing Data

| 2 | 41 | V116 | C73 FREE ELECTIONS |

"If a Communist were legally elected to some public office around here, should the people allow him to take office?"
633 1. Yes
413 2. No
16 9. Missing Data

| 2 | 42 | V117 | P73 FREE ELECTIONS |

"If a Communist were legally elected to some public office around here, should the people allow him to take office?"
450 1. Yes
588 2. No
24 9. Missing Data

The following 13 variables are measures of change in child political orientations between 1965 and 1973. They each contain categories like the following which reflect both the amount and the direction of change:

1. Up 2 steps
2. Up 1 step
3. No change
4. Down 1 step
5. Down 2 steps

The steps refer to the arithmetic difference between the child's code in 1973 and the child's code in 1965—i.e., subtracting the 1965 code *from* the 1973 code.

For example, in the case of party identification, a 1965 Democrat who became a Republican in 1973 would be coded "5." If that 1965 Democrat had changed to Independent he would have been coded "4." If he had remained a Democrat, he would have been coded "3." Similarly, a 1965 Republican who became a Democrat in 1973 would be coded "1." If he had become an Independent, he would have a code of "2." Finally, if he had remained a

DECK	COLUMN	VARIABLE	VARIABLE DESCRIPTION INFORMATION

Republican, he would have been coded "3." Independents, of course, can only change 1 step in either direction. Thus, their codes would have to be either "2" or "4."

DECK	COLUMN	VARIABLE	VARIABLE DESCRIPTION INFORMATION
2	43	V118	C65, 73 PARTY ID (V1 and V3 combined)

    34 1. 2 steps towards Democrats
174 2. 1 step towards Democrats
605 3. Same
205 4. 1 step towards Republicans
  25 5. 2 steps towards Republicans
  19 9. Missing Data

| 2 | 44 | V119 | C65, 73 PRES PREF (V5 and V7 combined) |

  60 1. Republican in 1964, Democrat in 1972
516 2. Same party, 1964 and 1972
346 3. Democrat in 1964, Republican in 1972
140 9. Missing Data

| 2 | 45 | V120 | C65, 73 CONSERV PARTY (V9 and V11 combined) |

  32 1. 2 steps towards Democrats conservative
  82 2. 1 step towards Democrats conservative
567 3. Same
218 4. 1 step towards Republicans conservative
  78 5. 2 steps towards Republicans conservative
  85 9. Missing Data

| 2 | 46 | V121 | C65,73 BEST GOV (V13 and V15 combined) |

  52 1. 2 steps more national
  42 2. 1 step more national
470 3. Same
150 4. 1 step more local
326 5. 2 steps more local
  22 9. Missing Data

| 2 | 47 | V122 | C65,73 INTEGRATION (V17 and V19 combined) |

  73 1. 2 steps towards pro
  75 2. 1 step towards pro

			447 3. Same
			126 4. 1 step towards anti
			201 5. 2 steps towards anti
			140 9. Missing Data
2	48	V123	C65,73 PRAYER (V21 and V23 combined)
			85 1. 2 steps towards pro
			33 2. 1 step towards pro
			556 3. Same
			22 4. 1 step towards anti
			119 5. 2 steps towards anti
			247 9. Missing Data
2	49	V124	C65, 73 TOLERANCE (V25 and V27 combined)
			4 1. 2 steps less tolerant
			93 2. 1 step less tolerant
			581 3. Same
			335 4. 1 step more tolerant
			30 5. 2 steps more tolerant
			19 9. Missing Data
2	50	V125	C65, 73 TRUST GOV (V33 and V35 combined)
			7 1. 2 steps more trusting
			72 2. 1 step more trusting
			411 3. Same
			436 4. 1 step less trusting
			124 5. 2 steps less trusting
			12 9. Missing Data
2	51	V126	C65,73 ALL OR FEW (V45 and V47 combined)
			30 1. 2 steps to all
			5 2. 1 step to all
			451 3. Same
			58 4. 1 step to few
			479 5. 2 steps to few
			39 9. Missing Data
2	52	V127	C65, 73 CYNICISM (V49 and V51 combined)
			5 1. 2 steps less cynical
			58 2. 1 step less cynical
			300 3. Same
			380 4. 1 step more cynical
			218 5. 2 steps more cynical
			101 9. Missing Data

DECK	COLUMN	VARIABLE	VARIABLE DESCRIPTION INFORMATION

2   53   V128   C65, 73 INTEREST (V53 and V55 combined)

      28 1. Up 2 steps
   264 2. Up 1 step
   553 3. Same
   190 4. Down 1 step
    26 5. Down 2 steps
     1 9. Missing Data

2   54   V129   C65, 73 LOCALISM (V57 and V59 combined)

    24 1. 2 steps less local
    67 2. 1 step less local
   365 3. Same
   135 4. 1 step more local
    42 5. 2 steps more local
   429 9. Missing Data

2   55   V130   C65, 73 EFFICACY (V65 and V67 combined)

    43 1. 2 steps less efficacious
   293 2. 1 step less efficacious
   495 3. Same
   196 4. 1 step more efficacious
    19 5. 2 steps more efficacious
    16 9. Missing Data

2   56   V131   C73 CLOSENESS TO M
"How close would you say you are to your mother?"

   451 1. Very close
   348 2. Pretty close
    59 3. Not very close
   204 9. Missing Data

2   57   V132   C73 CLOSENESS TO F
"How close would you say you are to your father?"

   340 1. Very close
   349 2. Pretty close
    90 3. Not very close
   283 9. Missing Data

2   58   V133   C73 CLOSENESS TO P'S
Closeness of respondent to both parents.

   268 1. Very close to both
   158 2. Pretty close to both
   247 3. Medium
    55 4. Slightly distant from both

DECK	COLUMN	VARIABLE	VARIABLE DESCRIPTION INFORMATION

			27 5. Very distant from both 307 9. Missing Data
2	59	V134	C65,C73 REGIONAL MOVE Whether or not respondent moved from one region to another between 1965 and 1973. 225 1. Stayed in the South 47 2. South to North 77 3. North to South 713 4. Stayed in the North 0 9. Missing Data
2	60	V135	C73,P73 FAM INCOME GAP Difference between family income of parent and family income of parent's child in 1973. 169 1. Parent lower 329 2. Parent and child same 292 3. Parent higher 272 9. Missing Data
2	61	V136	C73, P73 CLASS MOBILITY Difference between perceived social class of parent and that of child in 1973. 217 1. P working class, C working class 118 2. P middle class, C working class 181 3. P working class, C middle class 293 4. P middle class, C middle class 253 9. Missing Data The following 2 variables are measures of the difference in educational level of parents and their children in 1973. The "step" concept is similar to that used above (V118-V130), except that an extra step has been added to allow for the four different categories in the education variables. Of course "3 steps less" is not possible with the Jennings data because all respondents in the child generation were high school seniors in 1965.
2	62	V137	C73,P73 EDUCATION GAP The difference in the education of the "head of the household"—father, father substitute, or mother if these are absent— and that of the child.

DECK	COLUMN	VARIABLE	VARIABLE DESCRIPTION INFORMATION

<table>
<tr><td></td><td></td><td></td><td>6</td><td>1. Child 2 steps less education</td></tr>
<tr><td></td><td></td><td></td><td>27</td><td>2. Child 1 step less education</td></tr>
<tr><td></td><td></td><td></td><td>340</td><td>3. Same</td></tr>
<tr><td></td><td></td><td></td><td>260</td><td>4. Child 1 step more education</td></tr>
<tr><td></td><td></td><td></td><td>316</td><td>5. Child 2 steps more education</td></tr>
<tr><td></td><td></td><td></td><td>104</td><td>6. Child 3 steps more education</td></tr>
<tr><td></td><td></td><td></td><td>9</td><td>9. Missing Data</td></tr>
</table>

2   63   V138   C73,P73 MATCHED ED GAP

The difference in the education of the parent and the child of the same sex—i.e., mother compared with daughter and father with son.

<table>
<tr><td>4</td><td>1. Child 2 steps less education</td></tr>
<tr><td>26</td><td>2. Child 1 step less education</td></tr>
<tr><td>316</td><td>3. Same</td></tr>
<tr><td>212</td><td>4. Child 1 step more education</td></tr>
<tr><td>353</td><td>5. Child 2 steps more education</td></tr>
<tr><td>87</td><td>6. Child 3 steps more education</td></tr>
<tr><td>64</td><td>9. Missing Data</td></tr>
</table>

DECK	COLUMN	VARIABLE	VARIABLE DESCRIPTION INFORMATION
2	64-74		BLANK
2	75-78	V73	PAIR ID (unique number for each parent-child pair)
2	79	V74	STUDY NUMBER (2)
2	80	V139	DECK NUMBER (2)

82

APPENDIX

A. Note to the Instructor

This SETUPS package focusses on the role of parents in political socialization. The Jennings study is well suited for such a focus, because it matches parents and their children at two points in time. At the first time point, 1965, the children were high school seniors in probably their last year of intimate contact with their parents. Eight years later, in 1973, many members of the younger generation had established their own ways of life outside of their family of origin. The first time point allows a study of the transmission of political orientations from parents to children. The second time point enables us to determine how well the earlier levels of intergenerational agreement are maintained when the child becomes an adult.

These twin questions of transmission and durability form the central thrust of this package (Parts II through IV). They are not the only questions, though, which may be studied with our subset of the Jennings data. Embedded in the panel of parent-child pairs are data on changes in each generation over this eight-year interval. These data may be particularly appealing to a class on public opinion. Also contained in the data (see Deck 2) are measurements of factors which may condition both political socialization and attitude change—such as the strength of affective ties between parent and child, the nature of the child's experiences after high school, and key "demographic" characteristics of all respondents. These additional questions are treated in Part V, which is designed to provide interesting "leads" for research papers and other open-ended exercises.

The primary objective of this SETUPS package is to enable students to learn about political socialization, especially the role played by parents. Part II exposes students to the similarities and differences in the two generations' distributions of political views. It also introduces the variables contained in the codebook and attempts to stimulate thinking about the contributions of generational replacement to political change. Part III moves on to the individual level of analysis, concentrating on 1965 parent-child agreement in political views. Here, we infer parental influence from parent-child agreement while pointing out that such inferences may be misleading. The instructor may wish to dwell more than we have on the intractable questions of causality involved in inferring transmission from agreement. Part IV completes the analysis of the parental role by assessing the "staying power" of parent-child agreement into 1973.

83

Our examples deal primarily with patterns of parent-child agreement on party identification. This variable was chosen for two reasons: (1) It is prominent in previous studies of political socialization, thus enabling our examples to convey important substantive information. (2) Parent-child agreement is higher on party identification than on most other political orientations and serves as a benchmark against which to compare the other levels of agreement. Agreement on party, however, is far from total. This reflects failures in the political socialization process, as well as life cycle and generational differences in the importance of partisanship. Religious preference variables have been included in the data set so that the student can determine the level of agreement which is possible under the most propitious conditions for socialization. Religion provides an interesting non-political benchmark against which to compare agreement in *political* views.

The exercises in this package designate the general research questions and the operations which need to be performed so that these questions may be answered. Considerable discretion, though, has been left to the instructor or the student in the choice of variables. We recommend that students be urged to select different variables so that all possible results may be discussed in class and a broader view of political socialization acquired. There is also considerable discretion allowed in the choice of measures of agreement. Several different measures—percent agreement, adjusted percent agreement, Kendall's tau-b and Somers' D—are discussed in the text. To a certain extent, the choice of measures will be dictated by the statistics which are provided in the user's crosstabulation program. Beyond that, it has been our experience that the adjusted percent agreement measure is best for beginning students and where the amount of time to be devoted to the package is two weeks or less. On the other hand, for more advanced students and the advanced exercises of Part V, the correlation coefficients are extremely valuable.

A word of explanation is in order concerning differences between relationships in our data and those reported by Jennings and his colleagues. Even where the same variables have been used, there are three reasons why differences can appear. First, many of the variables from the original Jennings study have been recoded for our purposes by combining coding categories. Second, our data do not contain the sampling weights used in publications based on the Jennings study. Third, respondents had to satisfy two requirements in order to be included in our data set: (a) they had to have been interviewed in both 1965 and 1973; and (b) they had to be members of a parent-child pair in which both members were interviewed at the two time points. These two requirements eliminate 605 children and 928 parents from the original 1965 sample. All these things considered, though, the differences between what is found with our data set and what has been reported by the original investigators should be small and should have little effect on substantive interpretations.

A second, yet highly important, objective of this SETUPS package is to involve students in the process of empirical research. This objective brings

the student face-to-face with the computer—a confrontation which can be traumatic if not skillfully engineered by us and the instructor. We have recoded the data to make them easier to manipulate, attached descriptive labels, and provided a detailed codebook. The Inter-University Consortium for Political Research has provided the data in a form compatible with your computer configuration. Nonetheless, due to variations in computer environments, most instructors will need to provide supplementary information in order that students can make successful runs. Part B contains sample set-ups in OSIRIS II and III and SPSS for all the necessary runs and should be of some help. We recommend that the instructor provide set-up cards and output from a successful run to each student initially. Furthermore, because reading the output has proven to be the most difficult task in the exercises, the output of this successful run should be discussed in detail.

This SETUPS package, then, is designed to teach students about political socialization by involving them in empirical research on agreement between parents and their children. Not only should this involvement provide students with tools of analysis which will be useful in other settings, but we believe that it will deepen their understanding of political socialization beyond that which would be gained in more passive learning environments.

B. OSIRIS and SPSS Sample Set-ups

The following are sample set-ups in OSIRIS II, OSIRIS III, and SPSS for obtaining the parent-child crosstab tables for party identification in each year and then these same tables with controls for race—i.e. separately for whites and for blacks. For each table, the computer program is instructed to compute column and total percentages and the tau-b and D statistics, if available. The SPSS run reads an SPSS Save File which has already been created. (It is contained with the data set circulated by the ICPR to SPSS users.)

```
CROSSTABS RUN WITH CONTROLS (FILTERS) IN OSIRIS II ⎫
R=(1,1:3) C=(2,1:3) % = (C,TOTAL)¦STAT = TAUB*      ⎪
F1=(78,1:1)*                                         ⎪
F1 =(78,2:2)*                                        ⎬ OSIRIS II
R= (3,1:3) C=(4,1:3)*                                ⎪
F1 =(78,1:1)*                                        ⎪
F1 =(78,2:2)*                                        ⎭
```

```
CROSSTABS RUN WITH CONTROLS (REPETITIONS) IN OSIRIS III
*
TABLES
RACE      INCLUDE V78 = 1,2*
R = V1 C = V2 % = (COL, TOTAL) STATS = TAUB MDOPT = ALL*    } OSIRIS III
R = V3 C = V4*
R = V1 C = V2 REPETITION = RACE*
R = V3 C = V4 REPETITION = RACE*

RUN NAME      CROSSTABS RUN WITH CONTROLS IN SPSS
GET FILE      JENNINGS
CROSSTABS     V1 BY V2/V3 BY V4/
              V1 BY V2 BY V78/V3 BY V4 BY V78    } SPSS
OPTIONS       3
STATISTICS    6,9
FINISH
```

NOTES

NOTES